D1447186

You Can Survive College— We Did!

A Guide for Kids and Their Parents

by

**Beverly Parks Faaborg
and Tony Faaborg**

Dedication

To the Parkses and the Faaborgs

Copyright 1992

Beverly Parks Faaborg and Tony Faaborg

Library of Congress Catalog Card No. 92-071012

ISBN 0-932796-45-1

Printing (Last Digit)

10 9 8 7 6 5 4 3 2 1

Publisher—

Educational Media Corporation®
P.O. Box 21311
Minneapolis, MN 55421

(612) 781-0088

Production editor—

Don L. Sorenson

Graphic design—

Earl Sorenson

Artwork—

Clay J. Billman

Introduction

We wrote this book for you, our fellow college families. You, too, can learn from our experiences and have a smooth road through college. You will recognize people in this book because there are lots and lots of us out here who are traveling the same road. You will certainly recognize *our* family in these pages: a son who was the king-of-stuff in his dorm room, a son who was stranded in Atlanta, and a son who had to take physics twice.

You will notice that our examples and experiences are mostly *male*. That is deliberate because our family is all boys and that's what we do best at our house. Beside, we can avoid the clumsy he/she business! But, we guarantee that this book is equally helpful to girls and *their* families!

Our family has a mom who adjusted to spring breaks and a dad who survived campus visits. You will find yourself in here, too! Somehow it is comforting to know you are not alone and to know that your family also can succeed at college—we did!

About the authors

Tony Faaborg (the son) finished five years of college with straight A grades in engineering his final semester. He was a resident assistant with first-hand involvement in new student problems and regrets. Tony is an Eagle Scout and an officer in the U.S. Air Force.

Bev Faaborg (the mom) is a long-time educator and school counselor. She is the mother of two college graduate sons who provided in-house inspiration for this book. Another son is currently field-testing the ideas. Bev and her husband Phil live in Middletown, Iowa.

Table of contents

Chapter 1
Tying Up Loose Ends
(Wrapping up high school)

All eyes forward

When you can see the light at the end of the high school tunnel, and that light illuminates college, you are ready to prepare to attend your chosen institution of higher learning.

Is it all downhill from here? NO!! You have to apply to the schools of your choice, unless they recognize you as a hot prospect for some reason, and come to you. If you haven't heard from a college representative by the time you enter your senior year of high school, assume they will not come to you and you must therefore go to them.

Do you know how to do laundry? Do you know how to fill out the forms at the doctor's office? Where is your birth certificate? Which high school mementos will accompany you to college?

There are five concepts that ought to be high school graduation requirements for all seniors: systematically prepare college applications, establish a file of important stuff, sort stuff, meet the washer and dryer, and make the rounds of medical offices.

The College Applications

The hunt is on!

Applying for acceptance at a college is at best an ordeal and at worst completely mind-boggling. We will not pretend to be able to tell you exactly which institutions are best for you, but we will urge you to talk to your parents, visit your guidance counselor, and discuss your options.

Given the huge number and variety of colleges, universities, technical schools, and community colleges in the United States, obviously you should try to narrow your selection of schools before you start to apply.

Narrow the field

We recommend applying to more than one school, because you may in fact not get accepted to your first-choice school. On the other hand, applying to many schools can get pretty expensive—schools charge an application fee of anywhere between $10 and $100 to prevent people from applying to every school in the country.

Applying to three schools would be a good compromise: apply to one that you have only dreamed of attending (your "shot in the dark"), apply to one that suits your needs and that you would like to attend, and apply to one that you would attend only as a last resort.

Unfortunately, this strategy doesn't limit the number of available schools. This is where your counselor and parents enter the picture. Your parents probably have ideas concerning budget, choice of major, and even choice of institution; remembering that they simply want the best for you, listen to their suggestions and do not hesitate to make any of your own.

Make your counselor's day

After a preliminary (and by no means final) discussion with your parents, approach the guidance counselor and ask to see all the information on colleges in the United States. After your counselor

Beverly Parks Faaborg and Tony Faaborg

recovers from shock, ask for help in sorting through possible institutions for you to attend.

Counselors love to help, and they also love to administer interest surveys and informational questionnaires and do computer searches and help you wade through the volumes of printed matter regarding colleges.

To get the most out of these searches you should have a pretty clear picture of your personal "college profile" before you approach the counselor. Your profile should contain information relating what kind of institution you and your parents consider ideal. Consider factors such as:

- Distance from home
- Cost to attend (tuition, room, board,)
- Size
- Emphasis (Science, Liberal Arts, Technical)
- Entrance requirements i.e., minimum scores on *American College Test (ACT), Scholastic Achievement Test (SAT),* or class rank
- Majors you might choose

What will I be?

Choosing a major is sometimes the most difficult decision a college student can make. However, the decision doesn't really need to be made until after your first year of college.

First year classes are usually core courses such as science, math, and English composition; you could major in Underwater Basket-Weaving or Pre-Brain Surgery and still take these core courses!

Don't worry if you are not 100% certain which major is right for you. College students change majors an average of three times during their undergraduate days anyway!

Because there are so many majors to choose from, and because you will probably change it eventually anyway, simply pick an area of study that sounds interesting to you right now. Then set about the more serious task of finding a good school for you to attend.

We will discuss more about selecting and changing majors in chapter seven ("Changing Mascots...").

Go for scholarship bucks

Picking a school and applying to that school is just the beginning. You will also want to spend some time applying for scholarships, awards, and grants.

You may feel that the scholarships are out of your reach, but someone has to win, and your well-prepared application may win out!

Go shock your guidance counselor again by asking for every scholarship application available. Also check the various clubs and organizations your mom and dad belong to; many sponsor a scholarship program of some sort.

First, get a file folder

To prepare for the scholarship applications, start a file folder early during your last year of high school—actually this would have been easier to do three years ago if someone had mentioned it, but it's not too late to start now.

This folder should contain information about activities and interests you pursue, positions you have held in school and the community, and (in general) interesting things you have done with your time.

If some scholarship or award opportunity comes up at the last minute, all important information is right there in the file folder.

Most applications request information about your activities in several typical areas; in general, these areas are:
- Scholarship/scholastic achievement
- Community Service
- Leadership
- Hobbies/interests
- Character
- Awards received

Some items to include are:
- newspaper articles and photos
- awards for activities
- letters of recognition
- high school transcript up-to-date at the moment, showing grade point average and class rank
- certificates received

- list of activities so far (high school, community, church, and other) with year, offices held, responsibilities involved
- letters of recommendation
- a supply of photos (of you!) to include when requested

Put in a good word for me, please

The letters of recommendation mentioned here can be rather generic. They should relate, through specific examples, what a good person you are. Always ask for the letters of recommendation far in advance (even before you receive the application). The advantage of having the letters in your possession ahead of time is so that you can easily meet application deadlines, and no one is pressured.

Ask an assortment of people (teacher, employer, pastor, youth leader, friend of family, school counselor, principal) to write one for you. When you ask them, hand them a list of what you want them to include in their letter. The list makes it easy for them and also gets you exactly what you want.

Give different lists to each person according to their relationship to you; the more specific you are in your lists the better your letters of recommendation will be. Your lists might include areas such as these:

- Teacher: achievement, effort, accomplishments
- Pastor: values, principals, morals
- Principal: leadership positions, citizenship
- Employer: responsibility, attendance, getting along with others.
- Friend: character, positive family attributes

When you ask a prospect for a recommendation the conversation may go something like this:

> "Mrs. Jones, I will be applying for several (scholarships/ awards/recognitions/whatever) and would like to have a letter of recommendation from you. Would you be willing to write one and give to me? I will retype and re-date it and ask you to sign it each time I need to use it. I'll stop by next Friday to pick it up. Here is a list of what I'd like you to consider putting in it."

This list needs to have everything on it that you want Mrs. Jones to say in her letter. Don't be shy!

But I'm bragging!

When applying for things, or asking for letters of recommendation, forget modesty. The only way the reviewing committee knows people is by reading their applications, so tell it like it is and don't leave anything out, even if it seems trivial or that "everyone does that." Everyone does not "attend church weekly with family, usher at community theater, stay late to clean up after scout meeting, clean grandma's gutters, give blood."

Keep your list of activities and accomplishments growing in the file folder and look for areas that might need expanding before filling out applications.

If not much is filed under Community Service, for example, call the historical society and offer to volunteer, ask the community librarian how you can help, or visit the county care facility, the shelter workshop, or the political party offices.

Never, never send your only copy of a letter of recommendation with an application—you will have to ask the person to compose it all over again, and once is enough! Along this line, always keep copies of applications sent. You will begin to notice a similarity in them and you can use old applications to fill out new ones quickly.

Putting in a few hours on a weekend afternoon may result in big money in the scholarship game. Get the idea?

Start a File of Important Stuff To Take to College

While you are collecting information about yourself to use in applications you should also collect important papers that will help you prove you earned that scholarship, help you get a job, or help you get an insurance claim adjusted quickly.

Buy a red file folder

Store all of this important stuff in an eye-catching folder marked with a big black marker "IMPORTANT STUFF". This folder will save frantic phone requests to send or hunt these things, and will allow you to impress just about everyone with your organizational skills.

Here is a list of several things that you should definitely include in the folder:

- college acceptance letter
- applications or verifications for things like dorm room, job
- housing agreement for dorm
- scholarship instructions for use, how and who to bill
- transcript for college courses taken already
- high school transcript
- letters of recommendation and awards
- health insurance identification and information
- car insurance information
- birth certificate
- social security card
- phone numbers and addresses of relatives
- dates-birthdays, anniversaries of relatives
- charge cards information
- bank account numbers
- driver's license
- glasses prescription
- immunization record
- income tax information

Some of the records suggested here, like your birth certificate, social security card, or high school transcript, could result in much pain and grief to replace if lost. Put this hard-to-replace matter into a safety-deposit box and include *copies* in your "IMPORTANT STUFF" folder.

When you get your schedule of classes and your billing materials from the school put copies into this folder. Do this every semester and you will end up with a mini-file of business transactions with the college. If any questions arise concerning your records you will have ready verification and answers.

Sort the Rest of Your Stuff

As long as you are collecting scholarship information and important records, you might as well begin sorting the rest of your earthly possessions. This procedure is referred to by adults as "boxing up childhood;" those whose stuff is being sorted call it "throwing away my life."

The concept is simple: clean out your room and store or give away the things that have outlived their "meaningfulness." Although the concept is simple, in practice this task may create more friction among family members than any other aspect of college preparation; most of the friction will be over what you declare meaningful versus what Mom declares meaningful.

But those dried flowers are special!

Sorting your high school memorabilia may be exceedingly difficult while you are still in high school; you may actually want to wait several years (or as long as Mom can stand it) and then undertake the task. But no matter when you sort your stuff, you will have to make some basic decisions on where items go:

With you in your life's travels?

To siblings and relatives?

To the Salvation Army?

To a neighborhood garage sale?

To the dump?

The most efficient way to approach sorting is to get a disinterested third party to go through everything, but that can involve risk to life and limb for a stranger when entering a room containing a lifetime of kid stuff, although sightings of beds have actually been documented by volunteer sorters.

Three big piles

One method that works well is to gather a bunch of boxes with lids or tops, some index cards, and some garbage bags. Start going through all drawers, shelves, closets, and so forth and put everything into three big piles:

Pile One: Save Forever (mementos to show future generations: photos, medals, yearbooks)

Pile Two: Hold For Awhile (prom favors, newspaper clippings, graduation cards)

Pile Three: Discard (old t-shirts, school newsletters, petrified candy)

Expect that exercises in debate will occur as you and your parents make decisions about what goes in each pile.

When you finish with all of your stuff, or when people aren't speaking anymore, put things from piles One and Two into numbered boxes and list contents on a separate (similarly numbered) index card for each box.

Stash the boxes in the attic and keep the index cards at the attic entrance. The following week when someone wants to retrieve something, simply check the index cards to save crawling around the attic looking into each box.

Meet the Washer and Dryer

When you have boxed up childhood (or thrown away your life) you can feel free to learn some of the practical and domestic skills that will help ease you through school.

Have Mom and Dad teach you the basics about laundering, drying, ironing, and mending; they will love the chance to show off and you will learn several useful skills.

There is a myth among college students that sheets do not require washing. This is simply not true. There is a joke about freshmen wearing pink socks and underwear because of improper sorting and washing. This joke is, of course, based on fact. (Trust me; I know.)

Simple solutions to "The Washing and Drying Blues" involve either choosing only clothes of the same color which require no ironing, or buying new underwear when the present set has worn out its welcome.

College students of my acquaintance have attempted both solutions, and each resulted in a certain degree of success. However, the old standby, sorting and washing and drying, is still the method of preference for the vast majority of students.

The problems arise when you realize that you do not know how to sort, wash, and dry a load of clothes. Worse, you may discover a small rip in a seam or a button that has fallen off a shirt.

A few hours spent learning your way around the washer, dryer, ironing board, and sewing kit during high school will save much embarrassment later in college when you know not to wash that new red t-shirt with those white socks in hot water.

Visit "Fun Wash" with Mom

Sometime during the senior year of high school or during the summer following, thumb through the washer and dryer manuals, watch people doing laundry, ask questions, and then do some on-the-job experience until you are completely on your own in caring for clothing.

The procedure may vary for certain models, but the laundry basics apply:

- Have some kind of laundry bag to keep dirty clothes in (do your friends and roommates a favor and wash it too, once in a while)

- Sort clothes according to colors and water temperature required

- Treat stains before washing

- Select detergent and additives such as bleach, softeners, whiteners, deodorizers

- Dry clothes according to instructions (cool, hot, drip dry, line dry, and so forth)

- Hang or fold clothes—don't stuff them back into the laundry bag!

- Iron clothes when they need it (there is sometimes a difference of opinion between parent and student on the word "need")

Pay attention to care labels on clothing and also have some spot remover for dry-cleanables. You may wish to visit a coin-operated laundromat to get the hang of them.

Out, out darn spot

Eventually you will spill something on your clothes, or you will brush up against some wet paint, or someone else will make a mess of your outfit. Don't panic until you have tried to remove the spill, spot, or stain.

College students of ages past have discovered some ingenious methods for treating common clothes maladies, so you can ask around the dorm as well as consult the back of a detergent box.

Almost all stains like blood, grease, and food stains, will come out if scrubbed immediately. Wet the spot, pour on some liquid laundry detergent, and rub the stain with a brush or another piece of the garment fabric. Keep doing this and you will probably see results within a couple of minutes.

Insider's secret tip

If you should end up with a whole load of white laundry getting colored by a new red sweatshirt fading (Why oh why was that red shirt in there?? You learned to sort!!) There is a little-known secret way to whiten again. Simply buy a couple of boxes of *color remover* which is sold alongside fabric dye in stores, and follow directions for washing. This tip alone is worth the price of this book!

Pressing duties

After washing and drying, some of your clothes (especially cottons) will still look as if they had been crumpled in a corner someplace in your room. Now is the time for you to put to use another domestic skill: ironing.

Ironing is really quite simple. You will need an iron of some type, but you don't have to use an ironing board: you can make do with a chair or table and a big towel. While the iron is heating spread the towel on the chair or table to protect the furniture and your clothes; then strike when the iron is hot.

Even though ironing is easy, we have several warnings: if you see any spot or stain on your clothes as you are ironing, don't iron it—you could set the stain in the fabric for life. Instead, proceed directly to the laundry steps with that piece of clothing.

Also, be careful which heat setting you use! Polyester or other synthetic cloth will melt under the hot cotton setting!

Finally, don't leave the hot iron in one spot too long; you might scorch the fabric, which is the same as burning it, and fabric burns don't heal.

And can you sew a fine seam?

Once in a while a button will fall off of a shirt or blouse; most garment manufacturers don't do a very thorough job of putting them on in the first place. Before you are on your own make sure that you can do simple sewing tasks such as sewing on a button or mending a rip in a seam. The better you get before college the less time you will have to spend while in college!

Make the Rounds of Medical Offices

Remember that your dentist, doctor, and optometrist have college kids to support too; contribute to their cause by seeing them one last time at the beginning of summer. You can then follow up during the rest of the summer to get wisdom teeth out, warts removed, and contact lens prescriptions updated.

Have immunization records checked and get boosters if necessary. This is the last time you will be able to see the family specialists for awhile, so make sure to ask all the questions you can; and put any new material in your "IMPORTANT STUFF" folder!

Wrapping up high school is quite simple

There is life after high school! By following the tips in this chapter you have prepared for the beginnings of college life:
- Applications for scholarships and awards are done
- The "IMPORTANT STUFF" folder is ready for college

- Childhood is boxed up
- Got an "A" in laundry
- Medical appointments are done

The bittersweet feeling is not terminal. You and your parents, whether you like it or not, are starting a new part of your life: The College Years. The best is yet to come.

Notes to Parents

When your child is preparing for college, people begin to inquire as to his plans for his life. Avoid future embarrassment: Do not state emphatically that he "is going to U of Q, majoring in physics, and will work in a research lab for NASA following his Ph.D." Be vague and qualify all statements: "He is considering his options and is looking at U of Q, but we will see how it goes."

Do not brag about his lofty plans too soon because then people will want to know what went wrong. Nothing, in fact, is wrong. There are so many universities, majors, and career opportunities that chances are that the first decisions made will be changed—several times! And that is okay. College is a time of exploring. We parents should help the kids do what is best for them without concern about what the neighbors will think.

Although our children become adults, we parents are still the most important people in their lives and are their major support system.

As high school graduation draws near, relatives will begin to ask for gift ideas. You will need simply to pull out the following list and distribute it, but you could also act as coordinator to insure that there are not unwanted duplications. It is okay for the graduate to receive two towels, but he will hardly welcome two popcorn poppers.

Be specific about the graduate's preferences. i.e. electric, battery, or manual pencil sharpener with screw-down or suction bottom? dictionary from which publisher? fluorescent or incandescent desk lamp with clamp-on or with base?

Graduation Gift Ideas

desk stuff
pencil sharpener
note pads
markers
desk lamp
bulletin board
typewriter
computer
calculator
highlighter pens

books
dictionary
thesaurus
book of quotations
book of records
book of verse
Bible
almanac

bed stuff
sheets, pillowcases
blankets, quilts
comforters
pillows
back rest
electric blanket
lumber for "lofting"
    the bed
mattress pad

bath stuff
towels, wash cloths
bathroom tote bucket
toiletries
shaver
hair dryer
curling iron

food stuff
popcorn popper
hot pot
gift certificates for fast food places
plastic food storage containers
refrigerator

other
flashlight
brief case
book bag or tote
luggage
money
air conditioner
fan
bicycle, accessories
sewing kit
laundry bag
bus pass
book shelves
jewelry
duct tape
plastic milk crates
folding lawn chair
television
video cassette recorder
aquarium
telephone answering machine
pocket knife
postage stamps
coins for laundry
umbrella
medicine chest
sleep sound machine
clock

Chapter 2
First National
Bank of Bob
(The nitty gritty of finances)

A mini-course in economics

Next to their house, a family spends more on a college education than just about any other item or service. A well-planned four-year stay at State U for three or four kids can easily cost more than a house, and that just includes tuition, books, room and board!

Where does a family get all that money? Can or should the college student share any of the financial burden? How can families stay in the black and maintain friendly relations? Is financial planning necessary even if a family can already afford to send you to school? Families that do not ask and answer the questions surrounding financing a college education can expect to spend hundreds or even thousands of dollars needlessly.

It's really quite elementary

There is a true story that starts "Once upon a time there was a new college freshman who called home and said he owed $2314.89 by Tuesday and didn't know how to pay it." The story continues with drawn and wrinkled parents making phone calls and visiting various institutions, including mental, and ends with all learning a lesson in long-distance banking. You can prevent this from happening to you!

By the time you pack your bags for college, your family should be on a first-name basis with your friendly banker. That's why we call this chapter "The First National Bank of Bob." You should take Bob the banker to dinner at least once. If you aren't fortunate enough to live in a small town, drive to one with a small bank (and a nice banker) for the personal services you will require.

Sometime during your high school days, open accounts and set up your banking this way: One of your parents has a savings account and a checking account. You have a savings account and a checking account in the same bank, and mom's or dad's name is also on your accounts. From college you can then call a parent at work to say you need to have money transferred from their savings to your checking (as this is the direction it usually flows).

Your parents should have all of the account numbers written down and with them at all times. After your call they will then call your friendly first-name banker and say something like "Bob, please take $738 from my meager savings and put it in the Black Hole (your checking account)."

When you lose your checkbook Mom or Dad can call Bob and Bob will watch for unauthorized use of your checks. You couldn't get those types of personal services without Bob; that dinner will pay for itself quickly! However, be aware that Bob will sometimes call your parents with embarrassing questions about your accounts, too. For example, my brother Tim had to answer the rather embarrassing question: "Why did Thomas Jefferson sign one of your checks?"

We have the accounts, how about money?

Parents need not rely on winning the lottery to finance a child's education. One-fourth of the value of your house may seem like a huge sum to cough up (and it is) but remember that even starting with next to nothing you have about four years to find all of it. Ideally, your family should set aside funds long before you graduate. Even storing money in an old mattress (X dollars per month beginning your first grade year) is better than waiting until the last minute. However, we will not extol the virtues of investing money—most parents know that investing is an easier and more productive way than saving money in a mattress to build a college fund.

Let's say you and your family have about $10,000 saved for college. Panic time, right? Wrong; you are in great shape for now. There are sources of money you haven't even touched yet!

Student financial aid

There are three major financial aid forms: The Family Financial Statement (FFS), the Financial Aid Form (FAF), and the Single File (SF). After you fill out one of these forms, (and we encourage every family to do so), colleges will present you with "financial aid packages." The package will include five components:

1. The dollar amount your family is expected to contribute toward your education,

2. A work-study amount (a job helps you earn money to pay for school),

3. Any scholarship monies you are scheduled to receive

4. Any grant monies you are scheduled to receive,

5. Any loans for which you are eligible (you will have to pay these back).

The total of these sources of funds in a given financial aid package equals the cost to attend the college that sends you that package. We will discuss the various components of the financial package; don't be surprised if the amount your family is expected to contribute looks very large!

The first step in finding sources of money is to fill out one of three available financial aid forms previously mentioned. These forms allow the federal government to determine your ability to pay. This may sound crazy (as if the federal government can determine its own ability to pay!), but that is the way the financial aid game is played. Don't assume that your family earns too much money to be eligible for financial aid. Yearly earnings is but one segment of the form, and you and your family may receive quite a pleasant surprise when the colleges start offering you money to attend their institution!

The dreaded four-letter word: WORK

Some of the most productive resources are college students themselves. This means you! Once students have settled in at school a plethora of money-making opportunities becomes available. For example, every campus community has several businesses that cater to the college crowd. Not coincidentally these businesses love to hire college students. If you stop in at the nearby campus McBurger early enough (July is not too early) chances are a job will be waiting.

If you are eligible for work-study money you will have to apply for and be accepted into an on-campus job. Obviously, the college can't pay you for work-study hours until you earn them! However, whether you are eligible for work-study money or not, on-and off-campus work is a viable and productive way for students to help shoulder some of the financial burden of attending college.

On a larger campus, college students fill literally hundreds of positions in nearly every administrative and academic department. Students provide the college with a vast work resource, and campuses use students to paint, shovel, type, file, greet, and compute. Students putting in around 15 hours per week at an on-campus job can easily earn between one fourth and one half of their total college expenses!

What makes on-campus work more exciting is that often students can land a job within their own area of study. For example, biology majors may be employed as lab assistants in the biology department. On the other hand, sometimes it's fun to do something completely different—engineering majors working in the horticulture gardens or chemistry majors filing at the library. Most student jobs are not so specialized that an average student could not learn the job. However, if you stay with the department long enough (three years, perhaps) you may be offered a specialized job, fellowship, or even a permanent position after graduation! If you are early enough, you will be able to find an appealing and rewarding on-campus job.

Here is a hint: no matter where on campus you work, ask professors and "big-wigs" questions about their work, opinions, life. Most love to talk, and all have good stories to tell; after all, college learning doesn't begin and end in the classroom.

Scholarships and grants

Work is one way to make money for college, but you should also consider scholarships and grants.

Scholarships are awarded to applicants based on meeting criteria found in an application for the scholarship; criteria may include grades, honors received, membership in certain organizations, parents' place of employment, and so forth. If you meet the criteria better than all the other applicants, you win the scholarship. Here is where planning pays off! (See the information in chapter 1, "Tying Up Loose Ends....")

Scholarships are everywhere, from the local phone company to the megabucks corporation to the Armed Forces. Scholarships are where planning and brainwork in high school and college pay off. Many scholarships use financial need as a criterion; you must demonstrate "ability to pay" for college at or below a certain level in order to qualify for the scholarship. Attaching a copy of either the FAF or the FFS allows the body awarding the scholarship to assess your "need."

Grants are awarded (usually) based on financial need. If you qualify for and are given a grant you will receive in effect a gift of money to be used by you with no conditions or stipulations as to its use. You can apply for scholarships and grants in about the same way. Since scholarships are much more prevalent, for our purposes we will discuss more about them. You can adapt much of the information to grants anyway. Check with your school counselor for details.

Whether a scholarship or grant is given on basis of need or not the body determining who is awarded the grant or scholarship will require an application of some sort. Obtain an application (usually from the college financial aid office or your high school counselor, but sometimes from the phone company or corporation itself) and photocopy all of it. Then put the original in the Important Stuff file under "Scholarships/Grants." Then read the application a couple of times. Can you meet all the qualifications? Organizations giving scholarships have the legal right to be as picky about the recipient as they wish. For example, one scholarship offered at the college I attended required that the recipient live in a certain Iowa county and major in a specific area of study!

If you closely but not perfectly meet the qualifications, go ahead and apply anyway. You have nothing to lose, and maybe no one else has applied! On the other hand, if you are studying meat science and the scholarship is open only to advocates of vegetarianism then you may want to skip it.

You will eventually type out the original application and return it, but for now just write on the copy. This way you don't have to worry about mistakes and erasures. Using your photocopy, fill in all requested data. In areas like "hobbies," "leadership," or "community service," use another sheet of paper and write "see attached sheet" in the space. This way you get more room to tell of your glorious past, and you don't have to write the sections new with every application. That's a hint—most scholarship applications are very similar in format. If you have your prose arsenal polished and ready you can actually fill out most applications in just a few minutes. (Review words of wisdom on preparing applications in "Tying Up Loose Ends...")

Once you have finished the application on the photocopy, transfer all the information to the original. Always type, except where signatures are required. And be sure to attach all of the "attached sheets"!

One final tip: turn in or mail the applications as early as possible. Deadlines tend to approach and pass very quickly, and you may accidentally pass up an opportunity for thousands of dollars!

Loans

Check with Bob at the bank about loans. You will learn about regular loans that you start paying back immediately, deferred loans that aren't paid back until after college graduation (but sometimes the interest is due regularly while you are a student), guaranteed student loans backed by the federal government, and Parent Loans for Undergraduate Students (PLUS).

Your college and high school counselors may have more information for you, but consider first staying with the home-town banker. If you and your family's financial situation changes suddenly (your mom accidentally throws out the mattress) then Bob will probably be more sympathetic and willing to renegotiate than will a big-city, faceless financial institution.

Ask Uncle Sam: the military

The military options will not appear on any financial aid form, but the military offers a simple deal: money for service. You may not have seriously considered the armed forces as a way to finance college and serve your country, but you may want to investigate these options:

- Service Academies: Colorado Springs, Colorado (Air Force); West Point, New York (Army); Annapolis, Maryland (Navy and Marines); New Briton, Connecticut (Coast Guard).

- Reserve Officer Training Corps (ROTC): Air Force, Army, Navy/ Marine.

- Guard and Reserves: Air Force, Army, Navy.

- The GI Bill: Enlist and match funds with the government.

The service academies pay for everything. They also have a very structured atmosphere, and a demanding course load. You must obtain an appointment (usually from a US Congressman) to be able to attend an academy. The ROTC programs offer a variety of scholarships. Good sources of information for these options as well as the Guard and GI Bill are the high school and college counselors and the military recruiters.

The mechanics of moving money

Once finances have been earned, the question becomes how to keep you in school and keep your family out of debtor's prison or the Bad Credit Zone. It's easy for you to borrow money or visit the bank now, but how about when your parents and the bank stay home and you go off to school? Western Union may be the fastest way to send money, but it is also one of the most expensive. Automatic Teller Machine cards, checking accounts, and credit cards are convenient, but many college students find them a little too convenient, if you know what I mean.

With family needs and personalities in mind, you and your parents should sit down before your college freshman year and work out a financial plan. I'm not talking about how much to spend on what, but rather how and where the money will be kept. I guarantee that a good plan before college starts will keep problems to a minimum after college starts. You may come up with a novel and workable plan on your own, but here are a few suggestions for the mechanics of paying for college:

1. **"You're on your own, kid!"** You receive a lump-sum amount from parents to pay for tuition, room, board, and incidentals (see the next section); you may do as you wish with this money so you had better be responsible! The lump-sum amount may be distributed by semester, year, or even as one big lump sum for the entire time you are in school.

2. **"Mom, I need 100 bucks in my account by tomorrow!"** You call (or write) when an expenditure occurs. This way you do communicate once in a while, and parents can have absolute control over input!

3. **"Family, Inc."** You receive a salary. Provided you work to meet expectations (grades) you are paid by Family, Inc. accordingly. Garnishments or fines may be appropriate at times—remember, money is an effective persuader.

4. **"Family Bank and Trust."** This is actually a variation on "Family, Inc." in which you pay your own way for a period of time (usually a semester). After this period of time, if your parents' expectations are met (good grades) they reimburse you for that period of time. As long as you keep up in class, your parents foot the bill! Talk about incentive to study!

No matter how your family decides to move money, you will save Mom, Dad, Bob, your financial advisor, and the college a lot of headaches (colleges do get headaches) if you plan ahead for some of the surprises. You will easily be able to find out when the big bills are due (like tuition); the college will publish a calendar with all of those dates listed. With this information and with the family money plan you will be able to cut one of the largest spools of "red tape"—paying the college bills.

Incidentals

It's 11:30 p.m. and you want pizza. You are window shopping and you see the perfect party outfit for Friday Night. Incidental expenses, those not planned and often not entirely necessary, have a way of creeping into college life. These expenses should be expected to arise, and your parents will probably have some guidelines or expectations for incidental spending. For example, my spendthrift brother had to ask mom about every purchase he was considering over $5 in value! On the other hand, my parents never really worried about my spending; although I did raise a few eyebrows when I told them I bought 50 pizzas one semester!

Have a clear understanding of who (you or your parents) is responsible for miscellaneous spending money, clothes, phone bills, books, tuition, room and board, trips home, gas, credit cards, dues, lab fees, recreation, meals not included in room and board, personal items, club and organization fees, and postage. Discuss whether there are limits on any of the above. For example, long distance phone calls home may be paid by parents. Long distance calls to girlfriend may not.

I strongly recommend allocating a weekly sum of money for miscellaneous or incidental expenses such as toothpaste, pizza, snacks, and new underwear when the old set comes out pink. It is OK and often necessary (pink underwear) to spend extra money at school; however, spending sprees often end in financial woe or a trip to the Bad Credit Zone.

The first couple of times you do something financially questionable your parents will probably forgive you. But remember that you will not always have them to bail you out when things turn bad. Show them you can manage your own finances and you will pleasantly surprise them and start yourself on the road to financial freedom! That's a hint—later on, you will want to express your independence somehow; like, for example, moving out of the dorms and into an apartment. If you have demonstrated your financial independence your parents will be much more likely to take you seriously when you ask them whether you can move off campus!

Do I Need Insurance?

Your parents probably already carry some sort of insurance, and you are probably covered in this insurance package. When you move out of the house, even temporarily to attend school, you and your parents may find that the insurance coverages change. Look into your family Health, Property, and Auto policies and ask your agent before you leave for school. With the information your family discovers you may find it worthwhile to change agents!

Medical insurance

Health insurance is the most complicated of the major types of insurance, but your questions should be pretty simple to answer. You need to know if you will still be covered under your parents' policy even though you will be spending approximately nine months outside the home. Will you be considered legally independent of your parents during this time? Will the insurance company reimburse you when you visit the college town hospital? Your family insurance agent may actually recommend that you investigate Student Health Insurance, administered by the college. Find out exactly what will change about your coverage, and make sure that you and your parents understand the ramifications of the changes.

Something as common as a broken leg could eat up a chunk of the college fund if you think you are insured and then find out you are not!

Property insurance

Property insurance isn't quite as complicated, but it does have its own quirks. The main question here is similar to the Health question: although your stuff will no longer be under your parents' roof, will it remain covered for loss, theft, damage, or fire under their insurance policy? Insurance companies differ in coverage of off-premises property losses. One company may cover you regardless of where you live, as long as you are a legal dependent of your parents. Others may cease coverage as soon as you leave for school. As an example, one insurance company extends parental coverage to students as long as they live in school-sponsored housing (the dorms) but terminates coverage if they move off-campus! When you are talking with your family insurance agent ask where you will and will not be covered, and ask how to gain coverage if your parents' policy will no longer cover you. And don't think that by being careful with your stuff you will not need property insurance. You will lose your camera, or have your bike stolen, or find shaving cream in your compact disc player. Expect it, and be prepared.

Auto insurance

Auto insurance rates are figured based on three basic components: the amount of insurance desired, the type of car to be insured, and the driver of the car. The first two components probably won't change if you take a family car to school; however, the principle driver of the car might change! This is where auto insurance gets expensive. Newly licensed drivers and college-age drivers are defined as high risks by the insurance companies, and are charged correspondingly higher rates. If you are not the principle driver of the car before you take it to school, you have the legal obligation to report that change in status to the insurance company. Unfortunately, the insurance rates for that car will probably go up. Talk with your automobile insurance representative before you make any decisions; the best decision may turn out to be leaving the car at home!

If you will be taking a car to school, having an auto club membership for towing and other emergencies is almost a necessity if you don't travel with a lot of cash. With a membership, when you run out of gas or when your wheel falls off, you can get help without having to pay up front. I found out the hard way that tow-truck operators accept only United States cash. I tried everything else.

Life insurance

This may be the time for your family to consider life insurance for you. Most of the time life insurance is purchased so that beneficiaries may continue to live a comfortable life in the event that their principle source of income passes away. In your case, a small life insurance policy may simply cover final expenses if you suddenly go to your reward. You will probably not leave any large debts or any dependents (large or small), but the peace of mind of knowing that you have thought to take care of final expenses can be a great comfort to a family.

Notes to Parents

It's amazing how an offspring can have a higher standard of living than the parents who are providing the money! You can tell which parents have college students by the rust on their cars, the holes in their towels, and the peeling paint on their house. Planning ahead for college expenses should have started eighteen years ago, but sometimes we wake up and realize that, like Sleeping Beauty, we've slept through something. However, during the last months prior to college, be sure you get organized by following the suggestions in this chapter and you will be OK.

If you open joint accounts as suggested, you can bank by phone. Be sure you keep track of the transactions in detail. Tuck an index card into your kid's bank book or folder that you keep at home and record all transactions you make for his account. Inevitably he will call and ask if that $11 deposit was made or if you included the $2 (you owe him for calling home) in the deposit four months ago. He will have lost the deposit slips you sent and you will forget what you've done.

Sometime you will feel like the "First National Bank of Mom," as you keep track of transactions, especially if there are two or more college kids and some at home. i.e. Tim owes Tony $8 and Tony owes Troy $5 and Troy owes Tim $3 and Tim owes Mom... and on and on and on....

It can be convenient to have a checking account with a local bank in the college town but this can get really confusing if there's one at home with Bob, too. You can make that decision later.

There are other ways to get cash to Sonny, of course, but I highly recommend the Bob Method. You should gather information from your local Western Union office about their procedures and fees. (There are regulations concerning positive identification of the money recipient—he might need a photo i.d., but if he has lost his wallet again, that won't be possible. Sometimes a code word is used for identification.)

Some credit cards will do cash advances if Sonny is authorized to do so. Auto travel clubs sometimes will cash personal checks in their offices for their members. You might check out how to get cashiers checks, postal money orders, and such. Automatic Teller Machine cards might appeal to the parents of the one responsible college student in each state.

Maybe you can agree on an amount for his "generous monthly allowance." Tell him when he can expect you to deposit it in his checking account. Logically it will coincide with your payday and his needs. Realize that his needs will come more often than your paydays.

You might hear your child telling a friend that "money isn't all that important to me." Grit your teeth and don't shout, "then why have I been dishing it out all these years?!" You and I know that money is important to all, and we are going to get organized in this area right now!

Chapter 3

From "King of the Hill" to Cramped Quarters

(Housing)

Will your home be a castle?

After you have been accepted at a school and you make the decision to attend that school you will be sent lots of information about the many services the school has to offer.

Look over the pamphlets and brochures at your leisure, but right away dig out the housing information. Depending on the institution, on-campus student housing may be called dormitories or residence halls, possibly student apartments; prices should be included too.

Where will you live while you attend school? Do your parents have any preference where you live or with whom you live? And how will you furnish your living space?

You and your parents should answer these questions as soon as possible, because school-sponsored living quarters, as well as off-campus apartment and house rentals, are very popular and may not be available if you wait too long to sign up.

Housing Possibilities

There are many varieties, shapes, and sizes of student living spaces, but they all fit into one of four possibilities: The Dormitories, The Greek System, Off-Campus, and Commuting. You should investigate each of these options and select one to begin narrowing your search for a place to live.

Into this investigation bring several of the factors you used to determine which school to attend, but now apply them to your choice for living space: budget, travel distance to campus, size, and population, to name a few.

While most new college students select the dorms at least for their first year, we will describe each of the four possibilities so you can get a feel for all of the options available to you.

Beverly Parks Faaborg and Tony Faaborg

Option one: Dormitories

Most major campuses have some sort of mass-living arrangement available to students on a first-come, first-served, basis.

There is quite a variety in dormitories—at the college I attended the various dorm buildings could house from 50 to 1800 people, and they ranged in age from five to more than 70 years old. However, the living arrangements are usually quite similar: you may contract on a semester basis to live in a room that is about the size of your bedroom at home.

If you apply for on-campus housing you will most likely be served and assigned housing based on the number of people who apply before you. Some schools assign a "priority date," usually the postmarked date on your application return envelope, and you will be given preference over anyone with a more recent priority date. If your school assigns priority to early application returns then you should make haste in returning your application; you may not be guaranteed housing otherwise!

You will probably be placed with a roommate or two, and you may also be offered a campus-sponsored meal plan.

Dorms are usually maintained by a permanent staff, and each dorm room contains basic furniture: closet, dresser, desk, and bed. More will be said about the dorm room later, but for now compare the costs (room, board, space) and benefits (convenience, you don't have to clean toilets) with those for the other options.

Option two: The Greek system

Fraternity/Sorority living quarters are considered to be off campus, but they offer benefits (and costs) associated with both on-and off-campus living.

For example, your fraternity or sorority will charge social dues as their dormitory counterparts do, but Greek meal plans are usually more "homey" than the dorms, with sit-down meals and fewer people to cook for.

As with the dorms there is quite a variety in fraternity and sorority houses and personalities. Most are somewhat conservative—their members come from middle-class or well-to-do families, and the houses place emphasis on both academic learning and social endeavors.

Some houses are religious or ethnic in their traditions, and their binding ties of brotherhood/sisterhood come from this specific tradition. For example, Alpha Phi Alpha is a traditionally black fraternity with chapters on campuses nationwide that seek to preserve African-American heritage and provide support for their members.

There will be a campus office to represent the Greek system, and you should contact this office if you are interested in joining ("pledging") a fraternity or sorority . The office may be called something like Office of Greek Affairs, Greek Housing Office, Panhellenic Council or Panhellenic Affairs Office. Ask for information about RUSH.

There are two kinds of rush: formal and informal. "Formal" rush is the time set aside by the entire Greek system to actively meet and recruit prospective members; "informal" rush is less structured and a little more difficult to explain. If you have an idea about which Greek house you would like to pledge, and you know someone who is a member of that house, you may want to consider *informally* approaching the member to pledge into their house; this is the essence of informal rush.

Depending on the institution, rush may be simply a time to find out more information about the Greek system or it may be an integral part of the pledge process. In any case it is the first step toward joining a Greek house.

Joining a Greek house may present you with an interesting option: some fraternities and sororities do not require you to live in their house; indeed, some do not have a house at all! If you wish to experience the social atmosphere of a Greek organization, you may still be able to pursue your own independent living arrangement.

As with the other housing options, consider and discuss with your family the costs and benefits of Greek life.

Option three: Off-campus

Ah, the independence! You are your own boss, you don't live with 500 other students, and you can do whatever you want to do in your room—like cook, clean, and pay utility bills. Off-campus living definitely offers the best and worst of college life.

The variety of off-campus living spaces is much greater than that of dorms or Greek houses. You can choose to rent or buy outright an apartment, condo, house, or mobile home. And the living conditions can range from the posh elegance of a hotel to the pest-infested filthiness of a neglected junk yard.

If you want to live off campus and you want to get the most for your money you can save yourself a lot of legwork by starting your search on campus.

Most large campuses have an office or department that acts as a liaison between off-campus landlords and the college. Wise landlords buy into this sort of system because they know it's good publicity; on the other hand, your college will probably not advocate certain shady landlords and questionable properties. Check with this office to get information about locations and availability of units, and about the reputations of the landlords and owners.

Some colleges actually own several apartments that you can rent. In this special case the school is your "landlord" and you don't have to worry about the reputation and shady business dealings.

As we have said before, concern yourself with your budget and the costs, as well as the benefits, of living off campus.

Remember that a lot more responsibility goes with renting and maintaining your own place; you may want to put off this big step until you have established your good study skills and grades in college.

Option four: Commuting

If your family lives close to the college you plan to attend you may want to consider commuting. The important questions here are: do you want to continue living at home, and do you have reliable transportation to and from campus?

Commuting's lure is that it saves money on room and board; however, the savings may not be as great as you may think.

First, you will eat, no matter where you live; you can subtract food costs from the "savings." You will have to pay operating costs for a privately owned vehicle or for public transportation; subtract these costs from the "savings." Finally, if you ride in a privately owned vehicle there will be some sort of charge to park on or near campus. This cost may climb to over $100 per semester!

After subtracting these required costs from the "savings" you may find it cheaper to rent an apartment or live in on-campus housing!

Each of the four possibilities has varying levels of responsibility and independence; you will eventually have to make a choice between them to decide where you will live. However, we strongly suggest that you investigate dorm living first; you will be placed in a semi-structured environment and you will have a chance to perfect your study and organizational skills before you are faced with "real world" problems such as broken water heaters and irritable landlords.

The Dorm Room

Your dormitory room is an extension of your personality. That sounds like some interior designer speaking, doesn't it? However, the statement makes sense. Part of the fun of living in a dorm room is the challenge of turning a bare living unit into an extension of your personality.

If you love unicorns, rainy days and pastel colors, your room will probably reflect it. On the other hand, if you live for heavy metal and black, your room will probably not carry a message of unicorns, rainy days and pastel colors.

I have seen many different "looks" in dorm furnishing, and I am always amazed that the occupants started with the same basic room. Styles ranged from "Early Metal-head" to "Genius at work" to "Hot-Rods and Women."

If you have ever seen any movies where the plots concerned happenings on a college campus then you probably saw at least one shot of a college dormitory room. This Hollywood image of the dorm room is distorted from reality, to say the least. Perhaps the most obvious distortion to those of us who have actually lived in a dorm room is the size. Hollywood dorm rooms are huge! Some are like miniature suites, with multiple rooms! In the real world of college this is nonsense.

To get a feel for the actual size of a dorm room, stand in your bedroom at home and picture one or two other people moving into your bedroom with you. Space is at a premium in the dorm world, and those who do not learn to manage their space and make the most of it are likely to be cramped and lost in a room barely bigger than their own room at home. Before you continue with this section, please do yourself a favor and consider that if you are to be living with a roommate or two they may be planning to bring stuff too.

You will save a lot of grief and woe on the part of your parents if you contact your new roommates before school starts and coordinate who will be bringing what. If you all show up with a sofa each, your parents will not be happy. And at least one of the sofas will probably accompany parents home again.

The first consideration of most new college freshmen is what to put into their dorm room. Parents have probably given you two or three trees-worth of paper and pencils, and you probably received one or more dictionaries, thesauruses, and other reference works; what else is there? How about furniture? Will you be sleeping in your room?

The broad field of dorm furnishings can be broken down into appliances, furniture, and the rather ambiguous "stuff."

Appliances

Appliances such as popcorn poppers are not really necessary to live at school, but they are fun to have around; they give the dorm room a feeling of home.

You may, however, run into problems with the rules—some appliances, such as stoves or even microwaves, are illegal in some dormitories!

When you decide where you are going to be living at school, find out if there are any limitations on the appliances that you may keep in your room. Most likely you will not be the first person to ask about limitations and the residence department will already have prepared a list of "illegal" stuff that you should leave at home.

After you obtain this list make another list of those "legal" items you would like to have in your room. You, of course, have your own taste and preferences, but I suggest you consult the list found at the end of chapter one ("Tying Up Loose Ends") for graduation gift suggestions. (Don't feel you have to have everything!)

Furniture

Furniture may or may not be provided by the college. Most dorm rooms will have the basic bed, desk, closet, and chair; you will have to bring any other furniture you want.

Before you move your parents' living room group to school you may want to take a look at your new room before school starts. This way (while maintaining contact with your new roommate) you can decide what will fit and what you can do with your room. Most college students like to have some kind of sofa or several chairs in their room; then when (if) you have visitors they will have someplace to sit.

Keep in mind that with your college budget function is more important than looks. That ugly old couch Aunt Bertha gave you may be the perfect conversation piece in your new room!

You may actually want to wait until you have been in school awhile before you start to significantly modify your room. You can find plenty of old furniture in college towns, because other students graduate and still others simply never come back. My roommate and I had one couch that had moved from dorm room to dorm room for at least five years!

"Stuff"

"Stuff" is what makes a dorm room fun. Under "stuff" I place items like dart boards, extra sheets and pillow cases, and Nintendo (college kids love Nintendo).

You will notice that as you progress through college your collection of stuff will continue to grow. If you don't get used to passing stuff on to other students (Freshmen) or simply throwing it away you will find it taking over your life.

Sometimes I felt my brother Tim was the official Keeper of Stuff at our university. He always had new stuff "collected" from roommates and friends who were smart enough to unload it on him. He even admitted to rooting through the dumpsters at year's end in search of furniture!

Many people can't comprehend how much stuff a college student can fit into a dorm room. They should meet Tim. He eventually had so much stuff in his room that it took over his bed and forced him to sleep on a dumpster-couch.

On the other hand, Tim had a gift for furnishing dorm rooms. He could utilize every cubic inch of space, wasting none. His secret was milk crates.

You can do miracles with milk crates and the college student's best friend, duct tape. Stacked milk crates can become end tables, shelves, table legs and foot stools; what they lack in beauty they make up for in function. Their real usefulness becomes apparent during The Move (see chapter four); you can put just about all of your worldly goods into the milk crates and then pile them into your chosen mode of transportation! (You can fit 75 milk crates into the payload section of a pick-up truck. Believe me.)

Tim's lesson is to be creative. You can give your dorm room a personality, you don't have to live like a cave dweller, and it is possible to furnish a room with some of those comforts you are used to at home. You just have to be innovative, sensible and able to get along with ugly upholstery.

The roommate

Up until now we have referred to this mysterious living companion as if you know very well with whom you will be living, and as if you will be in complete contact with him or her. Unfortunately for you this may not be the case.

I have observed on several occasions that expected roommates may not even come to school! If you are planning to share a room with someone you don't know or have never met before then make all efforts to open and maintain communication before you head off to school, but don't be surprised if developments do not go as planned.

The obvious way to eliminate a lot of precollege roommate hassles is to pick one yourself. If you can find someone you know who will be attending your college then consider being roommates. This person may not be the perfect roommate for you, but consider the mystery alternative—at least you know about this person's quirks!

If you can't pick your own roommate then you must allow the residence department to pick for you. They will send you some sort of application containing questions such as "Do you prefer a non-smoking roommate?" They will try to match you to other compatible respondents, based on their applications too.

This is not the time to impress your parents with your high living standards. For example, if you smoke you will save people a lot of trouble by stating so on the application.

Before time for school to start your college might notify you of the name of your new roommate. Now do your best to communicate and coordinate! If possible your parents will try to arrange a meeting so you and your new roommate can get to know each other. Grin and bear it; it's for your parents' sakes as much as for yours.

Whether you like it or not you will have intimate contact with this person for at least a few months. At the risk of sounding like a sermonizing, condescending graduate, you owe it to your grades and mental well-being to try to get along.

You will have differences of opinion, you will drive each other crazy sometimes, but you will probably survive. Treat each difference as a learning experience—you will become a better person with each one! This is especially true if your roommate is from a culture different from your own.

You are now in-the-know

Housing in college is indeed a shock to many new students, not to mention many new "college-parents!" If you apply early and plan (with your roommate) what stuff to put into your living space you can minimize some of the shock. Remember that college students are supposed to suffer the cramped quarters; also remember that college students are innovative, resilient, and unique: make the most of your new home-away-from-home.

Chapter 4
When the Laundry Goes Home to Visit

(Breaks and summers)

The prodigal will return home

Just when you think you can't take another week of classes and weird instructors a break will appear on the horizon and give you hope. If a break does not appear on the horizon, and you are at the end of your rope anyway, plan to go home for the weekend!

Breaks and weekends away from school are great for recharging the mental batteries and just relaxing without the stress of school weighing you down; but some facets of these vacations can try your patience and will.

You are probably aware that you will go home for the summer, as well as for Thanksgiving, Christmas, and for Spring Break, and you might even be aware that you will have to move all of your stuff out of your room sometime to get ready for break. But did you know that your parents will still expect you to live by the rules at home, that you may want to get a summer or Christmas job, and that your parents may actually want to visit you at school?

The Move

"The Move" usually takes college students by surprise. During Finals Week in the spring students remember that they will have to find a way to move their worldly goods home for the summer, and they realize they cannot fit all of these goods into their friend's compact car.

The Move also has its counterpart in the fall—getting all the stuff up to school in the first place. However, for some reason moving the stuff to school is not usually as nerve-wracking as getting it home; usually students carry stuff to school over time, in several trips.

And here is worse news: getting all of the college stuff up to school in the fall and then back home for the summer gets harder each year!

The best piece of advice we can offer regarding The Move is this: start thinking of The Move before Thanksgiving Break in the fall and Spring Break in the spring!

If (when) you go home for visits or breaks take a load of stuff home with you. Take things home that you no longer need, such as out-of-season clothes or fans, or books.

Do your best not to return to school with more stuff than you went home with! You may think that old end table will look great in your room, but remember that you will eventually have to load your college life up and move it out, especially if you live in the dorms (where The Move happens every spring).

Time for a family vote

Even the best laid plans may not significantly reduce the mountain of possessions confronting you when spring semester draws to a close. Before the school year ends for good, hold a family meeting and discuss several options for getting you and your stuff home for break.

One option is for the family to drive two cars (or a pick-up truck or semi!) to campus and leave one exclusively for carrying your stuff. Another option is renting a trailer or a truck; this option can be expensive, however. Sometimes you can find someone willing to store stuff in their basement or apartment for the summer; this is where choosing your friends carefully can pay off!

Storing things

We have assumed that you will be able to find transportation for all of your stuff to and from school; however, you may not have this luxury.

If you choose to fly to and from school, for example, you will be severely constrained by the baggage regulations of the airlines. Therefore, you may want to investigate an option that is often better than carrying stuff back and forth at all: temporary storage.

Your own little warehouse

Business-types in college towns know that some people either cannot or will not transport their goods to and from college every year; these students need a place to store their stuff, and the business-types are ready.

Almost every college town of any size has a "U-Store-It" type of business, where you can rent a garage-like space for a period of time (usually by the month). With this leased space you can travel to and from school with very little effort, and you can be reasonably sure that your stuff will be secure during break.

The only drawback to self-storage in the summer is that usually the business-types consider rental for any part of a month to be worth an entire month's rent. Since school usually breaks in mid-May and reconvenes in mid-August you could be responsible for four months' rent.

The self-storage areas are usually quite big for one college student (even my brother Tim, the King of Stuff). If you choose to store your goods over the summer, I recommend that you find several other people to store their stuff with you. This way you all will have less to carry to and from home, and you can split the cost. When done in this manner, temporary storage is actually quite reasonable in cost when compared to the moving hassles it eliminates.

Going Home

You also have to get yourself home! If you do not have immediate access to a vehicle, check several types of public transportation for schedules and costs. You will need reservations much in advance of breaks at certain times of year, especially Christmas time but also Thanksgiving and Spring Breaks.

Hitch a ride—maybe

Most campuses have numerous public bulletin boards where students post offers of rides. Often you can get to within an hour of your home through the courtesy of someone who is traveling in the same direction anyway.

Must we remind you that there is potential danger in this? Check out the people in person and let them know that you are giving their names, addresses, and license number to your parents. Subtly ask for references and get the information for yourself rather than taking their word for it. Check their reaction to all of this.

You can get a ride for any break or weekend, but during the spring this possible solution has a severe complication: your driver will probably also be undertaking The Move! You may not be able to fit any of your belongings into the vehicle!

By the way, if you are serious about finding a ride home you should make a sign yourself and advertise that you need a ride. Post at least 10 signs around campus in heavy-traffic areas, and offer to help with gas, provide companionship for the long trip, clean the windows, and so forth. Be sure to leave your hoped-for destination and phone number!

Family adjustments

Now that you and your personal belongings are home for awhile, it's party time, right? Well, at least you will have the run of the house, right? OK, maybe your parents will actually not treat you like a little kid, right? Don't bet on it.

Your parents will certainly be glad to see you, and will probably roll out the red carpet and put your favorite food on the table; but you should do your part to make sure that your visits home do not result in those huge arguments and cat-fights you may have had in the past.

Something feels different now

When you return home after being away for months you will notice things about your house and your parents that you never saw before; rest assured they will also notice things about you!

College students, especially first-year students, encounter many new situations and fashions at school, and some of these are bound to have their effect on you.

Do your best to prepare your parents for any new attitude or belief you possess, or any fashion habit you have adopted! It would not be good for their hearts, for example, to discover upon your arrival home that you have decided to dye your hair green. Your parents may appreciate knowing in advance that you are now a vegetarian or even that you are bringing a friend home to visit!

Cultural shock for homefolks

When your parents voice concern over your new habits or style, realize that they are indeed a little old-fashioned, but they simply have your best interests in mind.

The first trip home for a freshman is almost always humorous; no doubt you will have picked up some styles and traits you didn't leave home with three months ago. Tell your parents that they won't be judged by your weirdness (at least by parents of other college kids).

Remember, however, that your parents have to continue living in the community and would probably appreciate it if you didn't get too wild with your attitude, style, stories, and so forth.

Emotional hazards at home

Ideally you and your parents will have discussed "Terms and Conditions" before you return home, but one of the first clashes with your parents will probably occur over The Rules anyway.

You no doubt believe (now that you are a college student) you deserve a break from those restrictive curfews and living conditions, and you are right. However, you are living under your parents' roof, and that means you will have to compromise.

For example, Mom and Dad still have their boring routines of getting up to go to their jobs, so something has to be done about the topsy turvy schedule of up-all-night and sleep-all-day. Help keep the peace by abiding by a sort of Quiet Hours time, or by making your noise elsewhere.

Other potential clashes lie in the vehicle situation, the telephone policy, and the dreaded curfew.

Your parents will not appreciate astronomical phone bills due to your talk with college friends around the country. They will appreciate knowing where you are and when you will be back; when you leave home for the evening, tell them your plan.

This sounds suspiciously like they are still controlling your life, but most parents can adapt to you setting the hours and agenda, if you keep them informed.

Everyone, including Mom and Dad, should leave notes when gone ("I'm at the store buying milk—back by 10:30") simply to be polite, not to show lack of trust.

Another surprising battlefield is the bathroom! If you live in the dorms at school, you will probably have the freedom to spend as long as you wish in the bathroom; sadly, you are not allowed this freedom at home. Remember as you meditate on the commode or undergo water therapy in the shower that you are home now and that others may be waiting for you!

Home visits do work out

Rules really aren't so bad. You are growing up, and if you can prove that fact, your parents will probably let up a little and stop acting so much like prison wardens. College is a transition time in growing up;

you are semi-independent when you attend school away from home, but you return and are once again under your parents' wings. When they see how much you are growing in courtesy as well as intellect your parents will be impressed, to say the least.

Employment Over Break

College students enjoy visiting home for awhile, but if they do nothing but lie around the house, boredom sets in rather quickly. College students also seem to be among the poorest people in the United States (by their own estimation).

These two reasons make the prospect of working over break especially inviting. If you decide to become gainfully employed in a job other than one you may have had in high school, consider when to apply, how many hours you are willing to work, your desired income, and whether you wish to continue to work during future breaks.

Be a jump ahead of the pack

Almost every college in the nation recesses for the summer around the middle of May. This means thousands of college students, all searching for a job at about the same time, descend upon the hometown businesses.

Let the hometown businesses of your choice know you are interested in work, and let them know early! You may even wish to consider summer employment before you leave for school in the fall, and thereby completely avoid the rush in the spring. Even if you begin your hometown summer job search during Spring Break you will gain a decided advantage over the other students.

How much cash do you want?

How many hours do you want to put into the job, and how much money do you want to make? During a break I like to do almost nothing that could be described as work, but I do like to have a little pocket money. For this situation a part-time job works into the scheme rather well. You need to combine your availability and your desired income to determine how much work you should put forth. If you need (want) a lot of money, be prepared to work for it!

Willing workers

Most bosses are flexible regarding college employees who can only work during breaks; unfortunately, not all bosses are. Happily though, some jobs experience the most demand during college breaks—for example, many long-term workers would like to take their vacation during the summer or during Christmas time. You can be available and you will probably land the job if you are willing to work during popular breaks like Christmas.

If you plan to keep the job, check with the boss's "flexibility"; keep your boss informed of the fact that you will be at school during a major portion of the year, but that you would definitely like to come back and work over breaks.

In a way, part-time jobs over break are better than "real" work. You can be assured that you will never have to do menial labor for the rest of your life; that's part of why you are going to college! And you can still pick up a few dollars to spend on yourself or save for your education. And there's always looking forward to getting out of the job and back to school!

When Your Friends Meet Your Parents

College students are portrayed as a rather nomadic group, roaming all over the nation in search of good times.

There is a little truth to this image, but more college students search for good food. While this applies more on weekends than on long breaks, rest assured that at some point at school you will begin to remember Mom's fried chicken or how Mom could cook circles around Food Service.

Go home with me this weekend!

Eager to visit home, and to introduce a friend to your home life, a conversation at school may go like this:

"I'm sick and tired of this place. I need a break."

"Wanna go home with me this weekend?"

"Well, maybe, but...."

"Hey—you can study, sleep, do whatever; and besides, Mom is a great cook!"

"Really?"

"And, this weekend is 'Taste of the Dark Ages' at Food Service!"

"What are we waiting for? Let's go to your place!"

Prepare your parents for the upcoming visit and make sure they understand that you will be bringing a friend (maybe several friends, if they hear the "great cook" part).

Tell your parents any requests for food, entertainment, or special needs your friends may have. Your parents will probably accommodate you on almost any reasonable request, but they need to plan for the visit.

Likewise, prepare your friends for the visit to your home. If your family has any special rules or traditions, inform your friends so that they won't accidentally fall into bad graces with your parents. Also, tell your friends what you plan to do at home so they can pack and dress accordingly.

When friends visit your home (and when you visit their homes) you will have a golden opportunity to expand your horizons, and that is what college is all about. You will learn from your fellow students and their families a little more about the world around you, and the social education you receive during these visits could never be learned in the classroom.

When the Parents Hit Your Campus

As surprising as it may seem, parents actually want to visit their offspring at school—at least once, anyway.

Sometime during your freshman year your parents will probably drop the hint that they would like to visit. Since parents are not usually good hinters, you will most likely hear something like "We'd like to come visit you at school next weekend. Would that be OK?"

At least parents give you a warning. Before they settle on when to visit, consider the following: timing, your living space, your friends, and what to do once they get to campus.

Make an agenda

If your parents want to see you the weekend before you have tests in four classes and a semester project due in another, or if your living area is planning the party of the year that weekend, inform Mom and Dad that the timing may not work out for you. Parents are pretty understanding about your busy schedule, so you may wish to work them in and let them know when you are available to receive them.

Sort the clutter

When you settle on the date for them to visit, plan to spend a few hours cleaning your room. This is not only to show off how well Mom has taught you, but also to cover your hide!

You may be surprised at what your parents will find offensive in your room; for example, if you have beer cans all over the place, they might get a bad impression about you, and that would not be good for your future.

If you have cleaned the room to your satisfaction but are still not sure Mom would approve, have a female friend inspect your living area for "offensive content" (trust me on this one—it works).

Prompt your friends

Most of your friends will have parents, so they will understand how you feel about yours visiting. Don't be afraid to tell your roommate and close friends how you would like them to behave while your parents are at school; your friends know that you will return the favor when their parents visit! On the other hand, don't worry too much about how your friends will affect your parents' impressions of you. They will probably still love you anyway.

Keep busy

Plan a schedule of things to do when your parents arrive so that they don't end up spending all of their time looking for offensive matter in your room.

Most parents would like to see the campus and the buildings you have classes in; you may even want to guide a walking tour complete with history and interesting campus information.

If possible, introduce your parents to the various campus staff people with whom you interact, such as your Resident Assistant, administrative staff, or even your professors! (Professors love the attention.)

While you are planning the schedule, think of what you would like your parents to bring or wear when they visit, and tell them in advance. That way you can avoid the embarrassment of Dad showing up in flowered Bermuda shorts and black socks with white dress shoes.

Make your parents proud

Don't be terrified at the prospect of Mom and Dad seeing your college room and friends. Your parents know that college is a sort of "different" place, and they already trust you to be away from them. Treat their visit as an honor to you; they are willing to take time out from their busy schedules to experience part of your life! And you can always get back at them by letting them experience Food Service.

Away From Home Over Break

Home may be where the heart is, but for the college student home may not be where the excitement is.

Sometime during your college days you will want to travel to someplace other than home over break; an obvious and over-commercialized example is Spring Break in the Florida/Texas areas.

It's a big big world

Some new college students go off to school never thinking that they might want to spend break somewhere other than home. This is the wonderful part of college education—you can learn a lot about yourself and the world around you simply by visiting a friend's house!

Your freshman year may not be a good time to try to take an extended tour of Europe, but you will probably be able to persuade your parents to let you at least travel a little over break.

While there are endless destinations and trips you may choose, we will discuss two excursions: the visit to the friend's house, and the school-sponsored trip. Both trips are relatively inexpensive and supervised, and therefore parents are usually quite willing to let their children take them.

Know thy hosts

Before you set off for your friend's house have him or her brief you on the rules, traditions, and so forth as you would brief them if they were coming to visit. After all, you wouldn't want to put your foot in your mouth at your friend's house—that would leave no room for the great cooking!

Over break you may find it easier to go home first and then travel to visit your friend. Before you set out make sure you know the way!! Plan your route ahead of time, and tell your friend and your family your plans and when you expect to arrive.

Maybe an educational trip will do

The school-sponsored trip could be anything from a class field trip to a club outing; however, all itineraries and plans will have the approval of the school in order to gain sponsorship. If your parents know you wish to attend a school-sponsored function they will probably be more permissive in what you do and where you go. For instance, I went to San Antonio for a week my sophomore year, and had a great time. My parents certainly would not have let me go on my own, alone, with no school sponsorship!

As with any of your outings, make sure you know the plans and that you inform your parents of your plans; give them an emergency number to call just in case, and tell them when you plan to return (and if they will need to pick you up any place). Do not be like the kid (my brother Tim) who mistakenly told his parents he was going to Minnesota with a college group and got there to find that he was in Brookings, South Dakota.

As we have said before, breaks and travel are golden opportunities to broaden your horizons. With a little planning and foresight you can turn a college trip into a pleasurable memory and a wonderful experience.

Notes to Parents

You'll recognize them from afar. They will wear worried looks. They'll have bags under their eyes, a drawn look and they will be buying milk. They're always buying milk at 10 p.m. and they'll be saying, "don't they ever sleep?? And the noise!!" Of course, it's college semester break and these pitiful beings are "parents with kids home." Plan for this to happen to you every three or four months for one half a decade for each of your 2.3 children.

When your son arrives home, immediately tell him that you're glad he's home. Gush, "it's SO good to have you back!" You must do this as soon as he gets home because it could sound phony after an hour or two.

When he first comes home, don't have a lot of things planned because he needs to unwind for a few days. Kill the fatted calf. Pamper him. Fix his favorite foods. Tuck him in. Let him sleep. Do his laundry. Respect the natural "let down" which comes after final exam.

When Junior has been home for awhile, you'll remember back to the first day he left as a college freshman and how many minutes it took you to adjust. "The bathroom's mine!" you shouted. "The car is mine! We have leftovers now! We have milk!"

There will be some noticeable differences with him home. Car keys are always missing. Plan ahead and have seven sets made for each vehicle. Buy extra clothes hangers because clothes come home in a laundry bag and go back to college on hangers—your hangers. Have extra bars of soap because the soap will mysteriously disappear from the soap dishes when he returns to college. Buy a water-conserving shower head prior to his homecoming.

Instead of attacking the person, attack the problem. Say, "We have a problem with the cluttered living room. What can we do?" Or, "We are running out of hot water. How can we avoid this?"

The first-time-home college student will be a fount of knowledge with opinions and answers for people's behavior and the nation's economy. After all, he has had one psychology course, and one economics course! Realize that you will not be able to compete with that!

When the college student comes home, it takes a bit of adjusting for parents to get used to midnight phone calls from other college students who are home and to all of the late comings and goings.

He's been on his own and now here he is back home—your little boy again. Hark! Think again! It will be real helpful if you reach an understanding about the car, hours to keep, phone calls, and quiet hours. (Remember that not all middle-of-the night phone calls are bad news. Kids quickly figure out the time zones and use the cheaper rates in the wee hours, so unplug your bedroom extension phone at night.)

There will come a time when Johnny will call home and ask your opinion about his spending break elsewhere. Don't take it personally: you simply can't compete with the allure of backpacking in the Rockies or working in the inner city. Look at it as part of his education and plan ahead for these trips when you're deciding about who pays for what during college.

Sometimes a cheap car driven to college and parked to be used for trips home is convenient. If two trips are close, taking one of the family cars in November for the trip home in December can make sense.

If parents are providing the car, decide if you are also providing the insurance and the gas. And is the gas provided only for trips home, with Junior buying it for any other use of the car around campus or other incidental trips?

Decide with your offspring who will be making all of the arrangements for these trips; if he is paying his own way at college, does that mean collecting schedules, making reservations, and getting himself to and fro also?

Bringing the girl-of-the-semester home need not be a nerve-wracking situation, but it usually is. Don't even try to learn her name. They'll all be from the same mold (petite blonds, willowy brunettes, outdoorsey all-Americans, and so forth) so calling her something generic like Dearie or Sweetie will avoid embarrassment for being one girl behind on names.

Tell your son the house rules ahead of the girl's visit. Suggestions: "Everyone has a separate room and everyone will stay in his/her own room." It's okay to say that you're old fashioned. "Junior, dad and I are uncomfortable when you disappear into the guest room with the door closed. Please humor us and go along with it." (Try not to think of the dorm rooms and closed doors the other thirty five weeks....)

Note: Moms will notice that stress-induced hot flashes increase during girlfriend's visit and miraculously subside after break ends.

When you wake up at 2 a.m. and notice that the guest room is empty, check the pier. He and Sweetie have taken a late night walk to the lake, and nothing more. Trust them! When you see a half full vodka bottle on his night stand, smell it. It will be his after shave. Trust him!

When parents visit campus, realize that anything messy, gross, illegal, or distasteful "belongs to my roommate." Therefore, do not visit at the same time as his roommate's parents or it could get embarrassing.

Be sure to ask what to wear (besides your worried looks) to the event or non-event when you are going to visit campus. (And be sure dad doesn't wear out-of-style clothes.)

Make every effort to be cheerful and positive and offer to take him and a friend out to dinner.

If you're carrying stuff up five floors to the room, don't embarrass him by sweating or passing out, and do NOT blow fuses or set off smoke alarms when using power tools while assembling shelves or lofting beds.

More that one freshman has gone home for first break without knowing when to report back. Be aware that you can call the admissions office or dig out the list of dates you got at parent orientation.

When he goes back after break, send goodies with him but remember the kids you still have at home; make them some nice cookies too—don't just give them the overbaked ones.

Semester breaks don't last forever and you WILL survive the cooking, smiling, and being nice.

Chapter 5
A Resort is Cheaper than Flunking Out While Partying—Part 1

(Making the grade inside the classroom)

Studying outside of class will prepare you for the tests, and you will complete homework outside of class, but the majority of grades will be earned inside the classroom. After all, inside the classroom is where the lectures are, where the instructor is most accessible, and where the (ugh) tests are held.

Three Keys to Success

When I was in my fourth year of college I developed Three Keys to Success in college. As a result of observation of others, discussions, and my personal experience I discovered three factors that can virtually guarantee anyone passing grades (providing homework minimums are met). The Three Keys to Success follow:

1. Go to Sleep
2. Go to Breakfast
3. Go to Class

They sound so simple, don't they? Now I give you the explanations.

Go to sleep

Go to sleep doesn't mean that you can put your head on a pillow for half an hour and count that as sleep. I'm talking about quality sleep here. You know yourself well enough that you can tell when you are getting the right amount of sleep. Don't sell yourself short! You will be alert and ready to learn all day long if you simply get a good night's sleep every school night! And if you don't believe me sit in a lecture hall sometime and watch the clowns who obviously didn't get enough sleep the night before. Do you want to be part of the show?

Go to breakfast

Going to breakfast actually has two benefits: the first, and most obvious, is the nutritional element. When you start the day with a nutritional breakfast (like the kind you see on cereal commercials, for example) you are charging your body for the busy day ahead. Don't skip breakfast! Even if you are not particularly hungry at that hour of the day at least drink a glass of fruit or vegetable juice, and have some milk. You must take care of your body if you expect it to last you through school!

The other benefit is less obvious: if you get up early enough to go to breakfast, and you get a good night's sleep, you must be going to bed somewhat early! This is very, very good for you. Most humans feel more rested, even if the amount of sleep is exactly equal, if they go to bed earlier and wake up earlier. Don't let people try the old "I'm not a morning person" routine on you. Most college students are not morning people simply because they stay up too late partying and trying to read four chapters of history in one sitting.

Go to class

Go to class. How easy can it be? Why do people skip class? Sadly, many students don't take advantage of the golden opportunity provided by class meetings (the ordinary, non-test class sessions). You too will witness this: people show up on test days who never set foot inside the classroom on other days. One instructor I know likes to point out these students. As he is handing out the test he says things like, "Have I ever seen you before in my life?" and, "Welcome to our class! We've missed you!"

Look at the skipping-class matter this way. If you pay $2,000 tuition for one 16-week semester, and you are meeting for class 15 hours per week, then you are paying approximately $8.33 per class hour, whether you attend or not. Would you enjoy throwing that money away? Consider skipping class to be simply tossing good money into the wind.

Besides the monetary consideration, you can't match classroom discussion and lecture for gaining true understanding of the material. You will have to put in outside time to put meaning into the material, but class meetings are where you "break the ice."

The Nuts and Bolts: Instructors, Notes, Tests, and HELP!

So now you have decided to use the Three Keys and succeed in class; what exactly does one do in a college class? For the most part, college classes are very similar to high school classes; however, we (and you) should pay attention to several unique aspects of the college class. First, the instructors change every semester. This may not be such a shock if you hail from a very large high school, but what is different about the college instructors is that you will know almost nothing about an instructor before you begin to take the class (especially as a freshman). Second, unless you have a photographic memory, you will have to take significantly more notes than you did in high school, and you will have to rely on these notes more heavily. Third, the tests will be more difficult. The format will not be especially new, but the questions will require more thought on your part. Finally, and surprisingly, you will actually have *more* resources available to help you succeed in the classroom!

The nutty professor

Let's begin with the mythical, tyrannical, eccentric, absent-minded, long-in-the-tooth, college professor. First of all, not all professors are scary! However, most differ from the typical high school teacher, and you should make yourself aware of the differences and of the quirks of each professor responsible for giving you a grade.

You will not learn these subtle things on the very first day of classes, but instead over the course of the semester. Find out what your instructors consider important in course reading material, and what they look for in assignments. Does neatness count? Does you instructor care about details? Are deadlines meaningful? Some instructors allow late work to be handed in, and others make the simple statement "Late work does not exist." Find out before you need to know!

Does your instructor grade your performance in the classroom? What about extra credit? Some college instructors actually offer chances for extra credit, but you will probably have to ask for it!

How do you find out what kind of lecturer, grader, and person your instructor is? The answer is contact. The more contact you have with your instructor, the more you will learn. Ask questions when concepts or facts are not clear to you; visit your instructor during office hours. If anything about the course especially concerns you (tests, for example) I urge you to discuss the matter first with your instructor. After all, this person is responsible for proving and underwriting your success.

I once had an instructor who came across in class as very short-tempered and impatient with students. She cared not for laziness, and was quick to reprimand even the slightest mistakes. Consequently we students were scared to death of her. No one liked to answer in class for fear of encountering her wrath; most of my classmates tried to look as if they were furiously taking notes on every word she said.

Then one day I realized what she was doing. She did not act in such ways simply to frighten us or to put us down. She was very "mission-oriented" and wanted us to learn the material—sometimes, we felt, at all costs! My entire perception of her was beginning to change. I decided to test this theory by visiting her in her office. She graciously (though quickly) answered my questions, and she actually smiled! Not one classmate believed me when I told them that!

This woman loved learning, and she loved knowledge. Now what kind of tests do you think she gave? No true/false, no matching; she was a concept (i.e. application, creativity) person. We had to prove to her that we were not merely regurgitating the information; we had to prove that we could use it. After this realization, I did not fear her, I learned what she wanted me to learn (after all, she held my grade in her hands) and my test scores went up. I did not cheat the system; I showed her what I knew, and that I could apply this knowledge.

The point of this example is that even if you know everything in the book you may still do poorly in a class run by a certain type of instructor. To do well in class means not only knowing the material but knowing how the instructor wants it presented, and how you can best prove to this unique and important individual that you deserve good grades.

Hey, can I borrow your notes?
I skipped class because....

Did you take notes in high school? Did you need to take notes in high school? How about taking notes in high school math class? In college you will find yourself taking notes in every type of class, and this note-taking frenzy will extend to your personal life as well. Don't say you weren't warned if you find yourself watching a movie and diagraming the plot on a pad of paper!

The first remark about note taking has already been made: *Go to class!* That is where the notes are! And going to class and taking notes are so important because that is how you find out what makes your instructor tick. You will be offered a look at what your instructor considers worthy of record—and be assured that most of this stuff will appear in some form on the test!

The very next note-worthy item concerns quality. You knew where this discussion was headed, didn't you? Do you (or can you) take good-quality notes? If you write down several concepts or points made at some sort of speech, can you look at your own writing three weeks later and understand the general meaning of the speech and its various points and concepts?

Many college students claim to attend class and take notes, and that note-taking doesn't help them study for tests. Usually, the reason is they don't take good notes, or they don't take enough (perhaps because they continually fall asleep in class). Over the course of a typical semester you will figure out how much note-taking is enough. Start by taking more than you think you should. Play "court-reporter" at least until the first test and you will find out after (or during) the first test whether or not you were too thorough in your work. However, no matter what quantity of note-taking you do, the quality of those notes will either make or break you.

How can you tell whether or not you take quality notes? Test yourself! If you have a chance, attend a high school class in a subject you haven't taken and pretend you are in college. Write down every bit of pertinent information, whether you understand it or not. After the class present your notes to the instructor and ask whether or not, using those notes, you could pass a quiz over the information presented in that day's lecture. If you pick a good instructor he or she will be happy to spend time with you discussing any details you left out, or even how you could have done a better job.

Six Strategies for Note-Taking

The preceding test is a rather easy way to gage your ability, but (assuming you wish to improve your ability) there exist strategies to note-taking that can save you time and increase the quality of your notes. The fist is our old pal "Organization," the second is "The Outline Method," followed by "Bugging the Room," "The Blackboard Consideration," "The Secret Code," and rounded out by "The Text Gambit."

1. "Organization"

This type of organization concerns how you prepare your notes for class meetings and study times. Just as organization is vital to your overall success and mental stability in college, so is organization of notes and class materials important.

You probably remember the annual or semi-annual trek to the "school supplies" section of your local discount store when you were in elementary school. You asked your mother to buy you one each of the latest designs of pencils, school folders, organizers, and book bags. Then in high school you wanted more of the latest designs, but needed less of the organizer stuff.

College will be similar to *elementary school* for you. When you trek to the discount store (do it early so you don't have to step on elementary kids) you will probably want to purchase one of everything because you won't know whether you need it or not. This is where "organization" can save you time and money.

College students are a little more independent than elementary school kids, so you will notice different organizational styles. This variety means that you can adapt the best features for your own use. For example, I changed classroom organizational styles four times during my college years, and ended up with a style that I think is the best anywhere. In this section I will describe the various styles and then tell you why I think mine is best.

One style is *"the magic book bag."* You can tell which students have adopted this style, because they will be forever searching in their bookbags for their notebook, assignments, pencils, and so forth. The book bag is obviously magical, because papers tend to disappear once inside. The style has one advantage: everything (and I mean everything is in one place, and all you have to do is find it. The disadvantages are numerous: assignments are usually crumpled and messy, you must spend extra time looking for items that may have disappeared due to the magical properties of the book bag, and once materials enter the book bag it is easy to forget they exist.

A second style is *"the big notebook."* Some people believe they can use one big notebook to take notes in all of their classes, so they buy one of those five-subject theme books. The method works very well for about eight weeks. Then one of the subjects becomes full, and the user is left with a dilemma. Do you add paper to that section? Do you buy another notebook? Suddenly the style is not as simple; you must realize that you will be taking lots of notes in at least one or two of your classes, and one notebook for the entire semester is just not going to work.

The third style is *"the spiral notebook and folder."* Students purchase a spiral notebook and a folder (cool designs optional) for each class. On each folder and notebook they mark an appropriate class. This style has its merits. You can dedicate a notebook to one and only one class, and you can carry an accompanying folder for assignments, syllabus, and handouts. The disadvantages are subtle, however. Instructors hate assignments done on spiral notebook paper. The hairy edge sticks to other papers, and instructors must fight the papers before they can be graded. Also, you can still run into problems by running out of paper before the semester is over. I had a few classes where I took over 100 pages of notes in a single semester! This fact isn't so astounding if you figure that in a typical class meeting 45 times per semester 100 pages amounts to just over two pages per meeting.

When I realized that I had to buy filler paper (the kind with three or five holes) to finish taking notes when my spiral notebook filled up, and to use for assignments, I hit upon the method I believe is the best. *Use only filler paper!* Buy (or "borrow" from your parents) a couple of big three-ring binders, at least two inches thick. Then purchase some "binder organizers." These sheets are made of stiff manila-colored paper, and have plastic tabs sticking out the side. Their holes are usually reinforced so that you can use them over and over again. Put the organizers into your binders, and write your classes on the tabs. You may want to split your class days in two so that you can use two (or more) binders. Now you need only carry to class this binder, several sheets of filler paper (I figure about five per class per day for "safety"), and your writing utensils! When your instructor hands out reading material or a syllabus, insert it in an appropriate spot in your binder. (You may have to use a hole-punch on the paper if it doesn't have holes already.) Now you have every piece of paper for one class in one neat, easy-to-access place, and you don't have to fight your binder or notebook every time you take notes. You can take note on a piece of filler paper and insert it in your binder when you finish that day's class.

I offer a word of advice here: put dates and page numbers and which class on every piece of paper that enters the binder! Then, when your binder unexpectedly opens and several sheets try to escape, you will have an easy time putting them back in order.

Whatever your chosen method of organizing for class, stick to it. Don't begin to slack off during the semester, and then realize that finals are just around the corner and you don't know where half of your notes are. You are organized in your daily life, and getting organized for class is very simple. Just do what works for you, and start getting organized early!

2. "The outline method"

Some instructors are scatter-brains. Others are so meticulous you can set your watch by their lecture format. When you find an instructor who is not too disorganized try to take notes in outline format. Most instructors include on the syllabus topics of discussion for the meeting days, and most also put down the pertinent chapters from the text book. (Remember to skim the text before class!)

When you attend a given lecture try to match the "flow" of the instructors presentation in your notes. For example, say your instructor is discussing reasons that the North won the American Civil War. He or she may tell you that Simms (an "expert" you have never heard of) states there were five main causes: Logistic, Diplomatic, Geographic, Demographic, and Economic. Your note paper may look like this:

    I. Why the North Won (Simms)

        1. Logistic

Why is there only one reason listed? Because your instructor will probably discuss this reason! Don't take a chance on running out of room by listing all of the reasons right away. This hint will help to keep your notes neat and coherent.

Your instructor will probably discuss the various reasons, and then offer arguments supporting or refuting these reasons. Your notes may look like this:

    I. Why the North Won (Simms)

        1. Logistic—able to move bullets, beans, bandage better

        2. Diplomatic—had more skillful negotiators

        3. Geographic—terrain made it easier for North to attack South

        4. Demographic—North had help from Blacks, other foreigners

        5. Economic—South currency not recognized in world market; couldn't buy anything!

    II. Support for Simms

        Text agrees with 1,3,5

        Instructor says 5 true

    III. Against Simms

        Text says Diplomacy failed, so wasn't factor

        Instructor says 4 made little difference;

        not as important as Simms says

Do you see how you can use your own notes to condense and simplify your own note-taking? Once you assign a number to a concept (such as each of the five reasons) you only need to refer to the number! This example shows how, in less space than one sheet of notebook paper you can document a complex argument between the mysterious Simms, your text author, and your instructor. By the way, don't worry if you haven't heard of "Simms." Your instructor may wish for you to digest only the reasons, not to dwell on the person. If your instructor doesn't think "Simms" the person is important, then you don't need to either!

The next step for you would be to make sure you understand why Simms discussed the five reasons, why your text agrees and disagrees, and why your instructor believes reason 5 and refutes reason 4. The outline form helps make a discussion or subject coherent and logical; all you have to do is understand the concepts and use your notes as a map.

3. "Bugging the room"

I hope you never have to face the following situation, but rest assured that you will probably hear horror stories about it if you don't experience it yourself. I knew an instructor who was a rambler. This instructor made no attempt to organize his notes, and preferred instead to orally travel from one subject to another. To make matters worse, he presented a variety of visual aids: overhead transparencies, chalkboard figures, and demonstrations. Most of the class decided that taking notes in his class was a worthless effort, since no one could make sense of his organization anyway.

What can you do in a situation like this? Should you just skip class; avoid taking notes; take down every word and then feel like you are beating your head against the wall when you study on your own? There are other solutions, and thanks to the wonders of modern technology you can maintain your organization and sanity even in classes as disorganized as the preceding example.

My first recommendation for you would be to beg, borrow, or rent a small tape recorder. This tape recorder could be one of those older (larger) models or it could be one of the new micro-mini-models with the cute little cassette tapes; just make sure that the batteries and the tape length will accommodate you for the entire class period! Then outfit it with one tape and take it with you to class. When your instructor begins the lecture, start recording.

Every time your instructor makes a visual demonstration of some sort, take notes on this material, and mark where in the lecture it came. That way you can match the demonstration with the oral discussion on your tape. You could mark the position in your notes with the meter number on your tape recorder, or you could say a few words into the tape recorder yourself, marking the same words on your notes. The tape recorder method frees you from having to write down every rambling comment made by the instructor, and allows you to concentrate on the visual material. These facts make the tape recorder method preferable even in organized classes, or when you find an instructor who is gifted in the art of speed-talking.

After class spend some time looking over your notes as you play back the tape of the lecture. Write down anything you consider meaningful, and simply ignore the rest. If you find that you don't understand a certain portion of the lecture then copy that portion down and approach your instructor with it the next day. Your instructor will either explain the material to you (and chances are other students didn't understand it either) or your instructor will tell you that the information is not important.

The good part about recording a lecture is that you can listen to the lecture at your speed later. Don't regard the extra work as a burden to you; regard it as a challenge that you can, and will, meet. And keep in mind that nothing in college is forever; the typical class meets for about 45 hours, and then it is done. Study your tape recordings after every lecture and you can count down the days to success.

4. "The blackboard consideration"

This strategy will seem obvious, yet you should know that some students don't practice it, and then wonder why they don't have all of the important information. When your instructor takes the time to write or explain some concept on the blackboard or on an overhead projector, you should realize that your instructor thinks this bit of information is very important!

If your instructor draws a figure on the board, set aside one whole page of paper in your notes for this figure. I guarantee your drawing, with the accompanying explanations, arrows, and notes will take up more space than you think. When your instructor refers to the figure directly, put the information in your notes; you can decide whether to simply write the information elsewhere and then refer to the figure, or to write the information as close to the figure as possible. Keep in mind as you take notes that this information, in your own handwriting, will have to make sense to you several weeks from now!

If your instructor writes a concept or statement on the board, copy it into your notes and then expect the instructor to explain what he or she has written. Most instructors follow an easy format: write on the board, then explain what is written on the board. But beware! Some instructors refuse to make their lectures that simple! Try to figure out early in the semester whether your instructor fits into either of these categories:

1. Write now, explain later: The instructor writes several concepts down, then returns to the first and begins discussion of it. Don't write down all of the concepts at once! Wait for the instructor to explain them and then write them down. You will have time to do this, because most instructors pause for you to catch up.

2. Write this, explain that: These instructors are sneaky. They require you to make connections between sometimes unrelated pieces of information or facts. You must think constantly! Don't simply copy down oral and printed material! Why did the instructor say this and write that? If you can't answer this question, then ask it out loud!

If you are blessed with an instructor who is an organized, patient, slow speaker, and who delivers lectures in easy-to-understand format, then you are lucky. However, watch out for those who are not so easy to follow!

5. "The secret code"

Have you taken a class in shorthand or notehand? Do you have the ability to write as fast as a typical human being can speak? Can you write this fast for 45 minutes straight? If the answer to any of these questions is "No" then consider learning some codes.

When you attend a lecture you will notice that your instructor tends to repeat certain words or phrases. When introducing a concept such as The Mean Value Theorem in Calculus, you may first write out the entire phrase in your notes. After this first time, don't ever write it out in your notes again! Simply substitute "MVT" or some other abbreviation that makes sense to you.

Remember, the only criterion for this "code" is that you understand what you are abbreviating and what the abbreviations mean. You may wish periodically in your notes (say every three or four pages) to write out the concepts together with their abbreviations so that you don't forget and have to wander through your notes trying to crack your own code.

6. "The text book gambit"

What if your instructor begins to discuss information covered in the text? Should you write this information down? I suggest not. By all means make a note to yourself that your instructor thinks this particular piece of information (found in the text) is important enough to discuss, but don't spend your note-taking time copying down notes you know you can find in the text later. Do copy down portions where your instructor deviates from or disagrees with the text, though!

I don't recommend that you take every text book to class every day, but you may wish to observe which instructors very closely follow the text in their lectures. It may pay very well for you to bring the text to class, and then simply include page numbers as references in your notes.

If you discover that your instructor follows the text almost exactly in lecture you may wish to try another approach. Start photocopying pages of your text, taking care to reduce the page to about half of a regular $8 \frac{1}{2}$ by 11 inch sheet of paper. Now you have your note paper pre-printed with the text book pages! When your instructor refers to the text, simply write comments right beside the appropriate page. Keep a highlighter handy, so that you can simply highlight passages your instructor refers to directly. Also have several blank sheets of paper handy so that if (when) your instructor starts to dwell on one particular subject or starts to ramble you can take notes without running out of space.

These note-taking strategies are the result of my experience in college classes. I know they work for me, and I also know they may not work for everyone and that not all of the strategies work in every class. However, keep these strategies in mind as you attend the first few days of class; you will be surprised at how easy taking notes really is when you use the strategies and you are prepared for class.

Hey; this study guide is like a test with answers given!

Some classes, especially freshman and entry-level classes, have accompanying study guides that either follow the text book or follow the instructor's presentation of lessons. The study guides provide further explanation of concepts, and offer exercises that students can do to practice the concepts and put them to use.

Usually these study guides are found right next to their accompanying texts in the bookstore. When you are book-shopping, make a note of any study guides available for your classes, but don't buy the study guide yet. When you attend classes on the first couple of days of the semester, ask the appropriate instructors whether they recommend purchasing the study guide. Most will have an opinion, and you will do well to take their advice. Some instructors even assign exercises out of the study guide!

Study guides can be very beneficial to your learning if you use them as a work book rather than a crutch. Don't gloss over material in a text book, hoping to gain understanding through the study guide. The guide is simply an extension of your regular study routine, and you should regard the guide as a place to apply your knowledge rather than a place to gain it.

The most beneficial part of using a study guide is that the answers to all of the exercises are given somewhere in the guide. The answers are nice to have when you are testing yourself; if you consistently answer questions correctly you can safely assume that you are grasping the concepts presented in class and in the text. Without the correct answers presented for you, you wouldn't know whether or not to keep studying!

Again, don't use the study guide as a crutch. Constantly referring to the given correct answers before or during the working of exercises does not prepare you for tests, and is not a good use of your time. Since you would only be hurting yourself anyway, try your best to answer the problems and complete the exercises without referring to the correct answers. If you can't complete a given exercise, look up the answer and then spend your time trying to discover why that particular answer is given. When you figure out the "why" you will have gained understanding of the concept.

Beverly Parks Faaborg and Tony Faaborg

Of dead animals and "cookbook" experiments: The lab course

Depending on the type of curriculum you undertake, you will probably find yourself in a laboratory-based course or in a course with a laboratory extension. I don't know very many people who think labs are incredibly exciting, but on the other hand, I know almost no one who doesn't like them. Labs offer chances to get dirty, chances for you to apply the stuffy concepts learned in a lecture hall.

Most college labs (at the undergraduate level, anyway) should be regarded as places for you to prove to yourself that concepts learned in the classroom apply in "the real world." Don't worry about Nobel Prizes yet; the lab assignments you will complete have been done by thousands of students before you, and your answers should startle no one. The answers should, however, stimulate your interest in the subject matter; or, failing that, should offer you a clearer understanding of it.

Most lab assignments come in three parts: the pre-lab, the experiment, and the lab report. You may be graded in any or all of the three parts, so don't mistakenly think that labs are all sharp objects and fire. There is quite a bit of writing involved, too.

Most pre-labs consist of a review of concepts followed by a few assigned exercises to help you understand what will be happening in the lab. (Actually, pre-labs are torture devices invented by college professors to make teaching assistants—who must grade the things—suffer.) Despite its obvious name, many students wait until lab time to complete the pre-lab! Don't fall into this habit; you will understand the experiment, and you will complete a better lab report, if you accomplish the pre-lab before lab time. That sounds obvious, doesn't it?

The experiment is the fun part. Here you may prove Newton's laws of motion, or find a frog's bile duct (it's the brown thing that looks sort of like a gooey raisin hiding under the liver), or you may employ computer technology to solve math problems. Whatever you do, take notes. You will probably be tested over some of this material, and you will need the notes anyway to complete the lab report.

The lab report is your proof that you accomplished the objectives of the pre-lab and of the experiment. Some classes have very strict requirements regarding the format of lab reports, so you should find

---

out the desired format before you hand in your report! Most formats require you to state a problem or objective ("Find the bile duct") and then go about describing how you solved the problem or attained your objective. Your notes will come in very handy here. Be as brief as possible (have a little kindness for the teaching assistants) but don't leave the important points out. Prove to the reader that you know what you are talking about and that you could perform the experiment again and obtain similar results. This, after all, is the goal of all lab activity.

A word about tests over lab material. Labs are designed to meet one or two broad objectives: One, you should come away from a lab with a more thorough understanding of the concepts discussed in lecture, and Two, you should know how to use the lab equipment. This second broad objective sounds rather trivial, but consider this: if you chose to major in chemistry, for example, your instructors would waste many hours of precious time if they had to teach you how to use chemistry lab equipment every single time you entered the lab! You can apply these two broad objectives to most freshman courses: you should come away with a working knowledge of the concepts, and you should know how to use the knowledge (or equipment, or laws and identities, or whatever).

And now back to the tests. When you approach a lab test situation expect to see some questions pertaining to the use of lab equipment. Instructors want to see that you didn't simply fill in the blanks in your lab report; the labs are easy enough that you could probably do just that, but instructors want to see proof of applied knowledge. Don't be surprised by "equipment" questions!

When your instructor has a paper with your name on it

This is a good time to discuss taking tests in general. This section isn't about preparing for exams (see Making The Grade Outside of Class); here we discuss the actual testing situation.

On exam day you will probably find yourself in a crowded room with other nervous students talking excitedly about some obscure point of discussion from a lecture three weeks ago. If you have prepared well (and I assume you have) then you should do your best to avoid the babble that precedes a test! I guarantee that this pre-test "discussion" will only make you nervous, and will not impart to you any significant knowledge.

Instead, why not plan to walk into the classroom approximately 30 seconds before the instructor hands out the examination papers? You will miss nothing, and you will be able to clear you head. Arrive a few minutes early, but don't go into the room yet. Take a walk around the hall, or even around the building; breathe deeply and enjoy life for a little while. You will notice other students in a panic trying to cram for that last few minutes before entering the room; they in turn will notice you simply walking around, and they will be amazed at your cool. This observation will only make them more ill-at-ease, and will actually calm you down! You now have a psychological advantage over the other students, and your mind is at peak readiness. You are willing yourself to succeed!

Once you enter the room don't blow your chances of success by discovering that you have left some important supply at home. Make sure that you have in your possession at least two pencils, a good eraser, and whatever else you may need: calculator, graphs, tables, ruler, protractor, graph paper, note-book paper, and so forth.

Although this may fall into the preparation category, find out before test-time whether your instructor allows students to use their notes, text book, or a "cheat sheet" during examinations. These tests are called open-notes, open-book, and (obviously) cheat-sheet tests. By the way: I actually once took an open-neighbor test! If you are allowed a "cheat sheet" you may have to create it yourself, or your instructor may hand it out with the test. Either way, make sure that you know what material will be included on the sheet and what material won't be included!

In college you will find all manner of questions on examinations. There will be your old friends True/False and Matching, as well as Fill-in-the-blank and Short Answer. You will also meet up with Essay Questions and the old-fashioned Exercises; and I must say that you will probably find more of these last two than you did in high school. College instructors for the most part like to mix formats up on tests; they seldom ask the same types of questions throughout an examination. Therefore, you should make sure that you can field any type of question that comes your way; if you are at all concerned about your own ability in testing situations you can consult with numerous books that have been written on the subject; find them in the library or in a local book store. The important thing is to do this before the college tests start!

Help ... Help ... Help ...

At some point in your college years you will probably feel that you are "going down for the third time," that you are not making the grade, or that you simply are not able (for whatever reason) to continue in school. You need to know right now that every student feels the pressure, and every student contemplates simply giving up. Take comfort in the fact that you are not alone in feeling this way; however, how you act and react to your feelings will either help or hinder your achievement of your goals of academic success.

The very fact that every student eventually feels lost, alone, and afraid in college has caused colleges to devote entire departments to helping students get back on the road to success. Unfortunately, far too few students ever take advantage of the services various departments provide, because students are either "too proud" to ask for help or insist on "making it on their own." I ask you which is better: Failing on your own, or Making it with someone else's help? I guarantee that people on campus and in your classes want to help, if only you will ask.

If you find that you are having difficulty in a specific class, the first person to ask for help is the instructor of that class. If you have been following the material and studying you probably have just a few concepts or parts of lectures that are confusing to you; therefore, ask the instructor to help you clear things up! Try to put your questions or confusion into writing; you will be able to better express your problems, and you will help your instructor to help you.

Don't be afraid to approach instructors! I have found that even the meanest instructors (now how can a lecture be "mean?") are really quite hospitable when you approach them privately. Just remember that, whether it's obvious or not, most instructors have your best interests in mind. And almost all instructors love to talk. And people in general love to help others solve problems, because it makes them feel needed. Just ask your questions and be ready to take notes.

If you feel you need more time than your instructor can give, consider obtaining a tutor for your class. I don't understand why people are so cowardly as to refuse help when help is available! Tutors can mean the difference between success and failure (and a waste of a lot of money); if you really want to succeed in school and you find that you are not doing as well as you would like to, I encourage you to look into the tutor possibility. Tutors are economical, they offer a different perspective on a course, and they can mean success in the classroom for you.

You may find that your difficulties are not confined to one class. If during your college experience you decide that the problem is within you, don't regard this as failure! You may actually have a physiological problem you didn't know about that is inhibiting your learning. Or you may simply be reacting normally to the stress of college life. Either way, don't make the mistake of refusing to talk with a specialist about how you feel. Institutions know that college life can cause a person's health to fail, and colleges have whole departments and counseling centers devoted to your physical and mental well-being. If you even suspect that you have some problem of any sort don't hesitate to talk to a health professional about it. Your good grades and your good health may be at stake.

After all of that positiveness, it almost seems a shame to discuss dropping sections and dropping classes, but they, too, are a part of college life.

I know several students who thought that once they enrolled in a class they had to stay in that class until the semester was over. Whether they understood the instructor or not, whether they had the ability to do well in the course or not, they thought that once their names appeared on the class list, that was it. I'm here to tell you that this just is not true. Almost all schools publish academic calendars, and on those calendars you will find dates noted with such phrases as "Last day to add/drop a class without extenuating circumstances" and "Last day to change sections." Before the specified dates, any student can drop a class or change sections for any reason!

This information is only included for your peace of mind. Don't panic during the first lecture of the semester and run out and drop all of your classes; instead, give the instructors a few lectures to make the courses and lectures appeal to you. Then, after you have given the courses and instructor a fair chance, and before the deadlines, make your decision: can you achieve academic success in this class? Would you perhaps achieve greater success in another section? Would changing sections, or dropping a certain class, be worth the hassle? Remember, if you drop a required class, you will eventually have to retake it, and that could change your plans for other courses too.

Think about it

The key difference between making it on your own and making it with the help of others has nothing to do with pride, honor, intelligence, or "guts." If you can achieve your goal of academic success on your own (both inside and outside the classroom) then I wish you good luck. If you realize that you would benefit from the help of others, and you use the resources that are available to you then I commend you for your honesty and wish you good luck.

Success both inside the classroom and outside the classroom comes down to you. What you do outside the classroom will have bearing on how well you perform inside the classroom. Make the most of your time, remember that the grades come first, but don't forget to enjoy yourself a little along the way.

Beverly Parks Faaborg and Tony Faaborg

Chapter 6
A Resort is Cheaper than Flunking Out While Partying—Part 2
(Making the grade outside the classroom)

Freedom to fail

College students are free. Unless you attend one of the military service academies or a heavily-structured private school you will be given free rein over your time. You will decide what to do with your 24 hours of every day.

The single most important reason anyone should attend college is to gain academic knowledge, and then prove it by "making the grade."

Students who would rather socialize should forget school and simply find jobs in a college town; they can make money and do all the socializing they want. Students who would rather protest, carry signs, or incite civil disobedience are wasting thousands of dollars; you can protest for free almost anywhere in the United States! Students who attend college to find a mate, "sow their oats," or "have some oats sown" should find jobs with the Socializers; it's cheaper than paying for college.

Freedom to learn

There is nothing inherently wrong with socializing, protesting, and mate-hunting; however, you must remain aware that the most important (not necessarily the only) reason you pay thousands of dollars to attend school is to gain academic knowledge. This is where the freedom comes in—after you pay your money, no one at the college will care more than you do about your academic success.

You will have the freedom to learn as much as they can teach you in the next few years, or to sleep all day and party all night, or to build your rap sheet by inciting riots and disturbing the peace.

In college your success is up to you.

Getting Organized to Succeed

If academic success is your goal you will want to hone your study skills and obtain tools to help you attain your goal.

To attain any goal takes organization; the emphasis in the college setting is often on time management. Given the 24 hours in every day you will have to decide how to best spend time to attain your goal.

Divide your time

I group the many facets of college life outside of class into five Fundamental Areas:

1. **Study**—preparing for class activities

2. **Work**—earning money or performing volunteer service

3. **Sports**—observing or participating in varsity, intramural, or individual athletic activity

4. **Extra-curricular**—joining non-athletic groups such as clubs, religious bodies, or student government

5. **Socializing**—partying, discussing with friends the existence of God, movies, and so forth.

The only college activity absent from the five Fundamental Areas is class attendance, and this activity is where college differs markedly from high school.

In high school you attend class for about as long as you sleep at night. Fully two-thirds of the high school day is gone if you remove sleep and class.

In college, on the other hand, you will probably spend in class about 15 to 20 hours per week. You will spend far more waking hours outside class than in class, and this is why you should pay close attention to the five fundamental areas.

How can you make sure not to lose sight of your goal of academic success? How can you balance your priorities? The specifics of a plan of action will be unique to you, but *time management* is the principle.

Time Management and the Ultimate Calendar Planner

Be your own chief executive officer

You can do what successful time-managers in corporate and private America do—plan your days in advance, make lists, keep calendars of events; in short, take control of every aspect of your life that uses your valuable time.

Set up a planner notebook

One of my favorite methods is the "Diary in Reverse" approach—keep a forward-looking notebook of upcoming events, tests, due dates, and meeting times.

While those expensive day-planners may look attractive and convenient, you need not purchase those glorified notebooks; just buy a small notebook in the stationery or school-supplies section of your local discount store.

Devote a back and a front page to each day of the week, including weekends. Make your notebook into a calendar by marking the date and day of the week on the back of each page. This way, when you open your notebook flat you will have one single day's notes before you.

Before marking a single appointment or test you are now more organized than thousands of college students nationwide!!

Include anything and everything

Now begin to use your notebook. Carry it everywhere; never let it out of your sight. Mark everything that may involve using your time; shopping trips, parties, tests, appointments. And above all, look at your notebook at least 10 times per day!!

Also look ahead to the next day's agenda; you will find it easy and eventually effortless to plan days ahead, when you have the events of those days already on paper in front of you.

Another key here is to leave reminders days in advance. For example, if some special person has a birthday coming up, give yourself advance notice. Notes in your notebook such as "Chemistry test Friday" on the Monday page will serve to keep your mind on what lies ahead for the week; you will not have to rely on memory.

You may wish to structure each day by the hour, but I have found in my personal case that this is usually unnecessary for the college student. The majority of your time-consuming tasks will not need to be performed at a specific hour of the day; therefore, pay closer attention to deadlines and due-dates than to hourly details.

Prioritize it all

This notebook should be more to you than a simple list of jobs and assignments. Personalize it!!

One of the best things you can do for yourself is to prioritize the day-to-day lists; keeping your academic goals in mind, number the tasks that lie ahead and then perform them in that order.

You can certainly block off areas of each page; for example, the left page may be "the important stuff." The top could be assignments, the bottom portion appointments. The right page could be "the non-essential stuff" such as party dates, shopping lists, and private notes to yourself.

Include class deadlines for sure

This is a good time to discuss the college syllabus. Most instructors will, at some point early in the semester, hand out a sheet listing the meeting dates for the class and what assignments or tests students will be responsible for on each meeting date. This syllabus is a very valuable piece of paper, and you should put it somewhere safe and handy.

When your instructors hand out syllabi (plural of syllabus) note on the appropriate dates in your notebook when assignments are due and when tests will be held. Mark this information in pencil; Instructors will always deviate from the syllabus sometime during the semester.

After marking assignments and tests, you will begin to see your semester take shape. You will know well in advance when your busy weeks are (usually there are a couple of "hell weeks" in a college student's semester).

If you wonder whether something should be included in your notebook, put it in! After a few weeks you will be so good at time management that you will be able to judge for yourself whether or not to include questionable bits of information.

One of the best feelings, when you have your notebook full of information, is forgetting things. With your notebook in hand, you don't have to remember all of the important dates and details of your everyday life. You will be calmer and less prone to stress. You will also have the confidence of knowing (at least for the next week or so) exactly where your life is going.

College is stressful and difficult enough; take advantage of every opportunity to make it less so.

Say No, No, No

Another useful method of taking control of your time is saying "NO."

So many activities abound at college, and you will be given a chance to engage in your share of parties, sports, discussions, pizza binges, and bar "death marches."

It is often too easy to say "YES" to invitations, and I actually encourage you to toss the books aside once in a while and practice your social skills; but DON'T become a slave to college society!!

Limit activities

I almost flunked out of school because I involved myself in too many activities.

In one semester I participated in Air Force ROTC, six different intramural sports, the university student judiciary board, I was social chairperson of my house, I tried out for the spring play, I ordered more than 50 late-night pizzas, and I had a girlfriend.

Needless to say, sleep and class took a back seat to my other college activities. After that semester I decided that change was in order (I kept the same girlfriend, though).

I dropped a few of my activities, and made academics my number one priority. Thanks to my attitude change and saying "NO" I made the Dean's List for three semesters following the one where I almost flunked out.

Be in charge of yourself

It hurts to say "NO." I didn't like the feeling that I was letting my college buddies down.

When I first started saying "NO" I also thought that I was going to have to miss out on the social side of college. NOT SO! When you take charge of your time, when you organize your life (such as with the aforementioned notebook) you will be amazed at what you can accomplish in the same 24 hour day given to everyone.

What's more, others will be amazed, too (that in itself is a pretty good feeling). You will have the ability to succeed in the classroom and still pursue the "fun stuff" that makes college such an exciting place to be.

Learning Outside the Classroom

Now that you have some tools to organize your daily life, you are ready for a revelation: in college, you will be responsible for learning more material on your own (outside of class) than you ever were in high school.

The cause of this phenomenon is a combination of business, economics, and sociology. The college has a limited number of professors and teachers; their job is to help educate you.

It costs money to hire these people, and therefore the college tends to spread them around as much as possible. What this means to you is you will likely have many more people in your college classes than you did in high school, and you will therefore not be given the close personal supervision and attention you may have been used to in high school.

What's more, the sociologists say you shouldn't need as much attention; you are maturing as a person and as a student, and you are quite capable of succeeding with only limited help from the "educators."

All of this boils down to what we said before: in college, your success is up to you. That doesn't mean that no one will help you! You have to ask for help, however. In the next chapter we discuss several places and ways you can ask for help.

However, for the most part, you will find that your success depends on what you do outside of class and on your own.

Learning Styles

How do *you* learn best?

We won't pretend that you have no idea how to study for a test, or that you don't know some of the tricks to answering essay questions; if you made it through high school and are headed for college you obviously have more intelligence than that.

However, you may want to brush up on those tricks before college, because every trick may come in handy at college.

Where did you study when you had high school assignments? Like most students you probably studied at home, or at least in some location where other people were present. Did these people do everything in their power to ensure your studying peace? Did they ever distract you? Was there a television in close proximity to you when you studied? Do you think that your study habits in high school will give you the college results you want?

The goal of this section is to help you realize your specific learning style, and to help you create an atmosphere where you can study and work to obtain peak results on assignments, projects, and tests.

Learning styles

If you prefer the following, you are a person who learns best by *seeing* things:

___I like to read

___I like a neat desk

___I like writing

___I like order and neatness

___I like to re-read text and notes

___I have an expressive face

___I make plans and outlines

If you prefer the following, you use your ears to learn. You learn best by *hearing* things:

___I like to discuss

___I like quiet

___I am distracted by outside noises

___I move my lips when reading silently

___I like speech and debate

___I like to listen to music

___I study for tests by having someone quiz me

If you prefer the following, you like to jump in and do rather than watch demonstrations or listen to lectures. You are a *hands-on* learner:

___I like "doing" things

___I like to move around when studying

___I use my hands when talking

___I need to be directly involved

___I like puzzles, codes, brain teasers

___I like to doodle, sketch

___I like to act

___I do not tend toward order and neatness

___I like a comfortable study area

___I make up sample tests to study

How can putting a title on the kind of learner you are help raise your grades? The more you know about yourself, the more you can capitalize on it when studying.

Your eyes

For example, a "visual" learner has to see it in black and white—on the chalk board, in the textbook, in pictures and illustrations. Taking notes during a lecture in order to "see the lecture in print" reinforces what you heard said. You study best with a neat desk area.

Your ears

If you are an "auditory" learner, you probably profit from tape recording lectures and listening to them over and over. You enjoy discussing the material with someone else in order to "hear it a different way." You might read your notes out loud to yourself in order to hear them again.

Your hands

A "tactile" learner excels in lab courses and hands-on assignments. You like activity, gadgets, and tools to figure out answers rather than doing problems in your head. The old test file or the sample problems appeal to you. You need to have a comfy study area, and take lots of breaks.

Know yourself

Now that you know your learning style, and you have the attitude for success, you are ready to get busy and start "making the grade."

Know that your particular learning style can be your downfall unless you arrange study time properly. For example, if you know that you must have peace and quiet to concentrate, then you sabotage yourself if you choose to study amongst friends. If you like to read the material over as review for test, then do not study with friends who want to discuss and quiz each other. If you like to get up and walk around while "reciting" when you study, then avoid the quiet library tables.

To succeed in college you will have to assess and revise your study habits, and you will have to find a place where you can get the most out of your study time.

P.S. Remember Flash Cards?

Do you remember when you were in grade school and you were trying to remember your addition or multiplication tables? Chances are you were then introduced to flashcards, and you and a partner spent a lot of time drilling each other on arithmetic problems.

Why did you stop using flashcards? Was it because you found better study techniques? Or was it because the material you had to learn couldn't be put on flashcards?

Most high school students think flashcards are too "elementary" to be effective past elementary school. The simple fact is that flashcards are so elementary they remain effective even into professional life beyond college!

Sometimes the only thing about flashcards that changes is the name: the more "advanced learning" cards are called "reference cards."

No matter what they are called, flashcards serve to illustrate that your study habits in college could really benefit from a return to the basics: constant review, drill, problem-solving exercises, and thorough reading.

Where to Study?

I thought high school was pretty easy most of the time. I could easily finish my assignments during reruns of *The Brady Bunch* and *Gilligan's Island*.

College is different. You will find in college that distractions and wishy-washy study habits will ruin your chances of academic success.

Be a hermit

Unless you study with a group of classmates who are also devoted to academic success, my opinion is that you will do your grades a favor your first few years if you find a study area out of the high-traffic spots, and away from people who do not have your academic success in mind.

If you find after a couple of years that you can study in the campus McBurger (people do study in fast-food restaurants) then I wish you well.

My study habits evolved similarly over the course of my college years, but I know that I would never have survived my freshman and sophomore years by studying in "people" areas.

Try the library

Where are the quiet study areas? You may try the library, but watch out: unless it is a really big one, you will probably find that the library is one of those "in" places to congregate.

People who want to "be seen" in academic mode go to the library; they talk with other socialites and effectively do nothing in the way of studying; they also ruin the atmosphere for those people you really go to the library to study.

If, however, the campus library is rather large you may be able to find several good spots to set up camp. Look for tables and desks in corners, in the back of the library, and in places people don't normally walk—the rare book room, for example.

Or look at a map of the library and find a set of books that no one ever uses; one of the best study places at the library I used was near the research papers, masters and doctoral theses! Not much through-traffic there.

The worst places to study in a library: by steps, by drinking fountains and rest rooms, and anywhere near doors or reference files. And stay away from the card catalog (when you *study*; not all the time).

Use empty classrooms

You might look for a quiet study area in other campus buildings and classrooms. Some campuses keep certain buildings open 24 hours per day; usually these buildings quiet down after 9 p.m.

Other buildings may be locked at a certain hour; if you get into a building before it is locked, you may be able to stay (as long as you don't cause trouble) until well after the doors are locked. (It goes without saying that you should use sensible safety precautions.) These buildings provide possibly the best opportunity for quality study time with few distractions.

Study off-campus

You may be able to find several off-campus buildings that offer quiet surroundings and a comfortable study space.

For example, several churches near campus should offer some kind of student work area and times when students can use the church to prepare lessons or study. Try these locations too, especially if you plan to attend one of the churches anyway.

You may want to try the town public library; usually the public libraries are nowhere near as busy as the college library, but they may also be nowhere nearby, either.

Prepare your environment

What about furnishings? What do you need besides a room and chair? A desk would be nice, but any flat surface big enough to spread out all of my stuff worked well for me.

Also you will benefit from lights. Good lighting is important, but students don't always know that certain lighting is bad for them until the headaches set in or until the optometrist tells them their eyes are going bad.

Whenever you can, have more than one source of light; multiple sources tend to reduce shadows.

Also try to find indirect light. This is light that has been bounced off ceiling or walls before it reaches you. Indirect lighting is best because it is softer, glare-free, and reduces or even eliminates shadows.

Make sure, however, the lighting is of the right quantity. Most students err in the direction of too much light, hitting their desk with light from a single 100-watt bulb three feet from their papers.

You can get along with less light than you think; while moon light or candle light may be a little extreme, try reducing the amount of light in your study area a little, and notice how easily your eyes adapt, and how much less strain you put on yourself.

Collect your materials

What should you bring with you to study? Here is where the previously mentioned organization begins to pay off.

I personally used to get enjoyment out of people who would trudge around campus with several textbooks, notebooks, papers, folders, paper clips, pencils, erasers, calculators, dictionary, and various other objects crammed into a bulging shoulder pack that certainly looked as if it would rather be elsewhere.

Sometime when you have nothing better to do put several hardcover books into a bag and walk around with this bag on your shoulder for half an hour. Would you rather look like the hunchback of Notre Dame or would you rather play it cool and use your great organizational skills?

You know from your precious notebook which assignments and projects should be occupying your time, so don't carry around a bunch of stuff you don't need!

If it's math for the evening, leave the psychology book home. Take plenty of paper, writing utensils, and any tools you may require, but don't weigh yourself down.

The goal here is to accomplish what has to be done (the upcoming assignments). If you carry a lot of different projects around you will more than likely forget something important (like the assignment sheet) or you will spend most of your time trying to decide which subject to spend your time on!

Some people will tell you that you may want to bring along something else to do in case you finish your assignment early, or in case you find some time you didn't think you would have. For at least the first few weeks of college, forget it. You probably won't find extra time, and you probably won't finish your assignments early.

If you do, celebrate! You are so organized and faithful to your studies that you deserve a treat! Go to bed, or send out for pizza, or sit around the dorm and laugh at all of the other students who wait until the last minute to do things and never seem to have the time to just sit around.

If you are caught up in your studies, just sitting around can be very healthy, I guarantee.

Attitude

Look around you

A final item to take with you wherever you choose to study is *attitude*.

Sitting in the library for three hours does not equal three hours of studying! You will only fool yourself if you believe otherwise.

One time I finished studying at the library a little early, so I decided to watch some of the other "studiers." One guy was definitely more of a socialite than a student. He sat at his books for about five minutes, then got up and wandered over to the drinking fountain. He said hi to the people he knew, then got the drink he was so thirsty for. He took a rather roundabout way back to his seat, pausing to look out the windows, and say hi to more of his friends.

I actually kept track: in one hour, he studied for 10 minutes! Rather, he sat at his books for 10 minutes. I don't know how long he actually studied.

I also had the pleasure of overhearing one of his conversations with a woman who was "studying" near my table. It went something like this (real names haven't been used):

"Hey, Bunny, whatcha studying?"

"I'm trying to get caught up in Psych, Biff. How about you?"

"I've got this major History test tomorrow. I have to read four chapters tonight! Can you imagine the nerve of that guy? Assigning all that reading on a Thursday night? But I have a friend who took the class last year, and he said that the old geezer doesn't test much over the reading material. And I can B.S. my way through essay questions. I should be an English major!"

"Are you going to be at our function tomorrow?"

"You bet, Bunny! Hey, are all of the Alpha Gams gonna be wearing costumes?"

"Yeah, we get fined if we don't."

"Bummer. Hey; what are you gonna wear?"

(and on, and on, into the night....)

You tell me: Do you feel sorry for Biff having to spend so much time "studying at the library?

What's wrong with this exchange? First of all, history professors don't assign four chapters per night. They are not that mean. Biff is just too lazy and insecure to admit that he put off the reading until the night before the test. Bunny and Biff also seem to be more interested in the "function" Friday night than in their upcoming examinations. Why are they at the library? Couldn't this exchange have occurred over the telephone?

The answer is attitude. Biff likes to be perceived as a studious person; he hangs out at the library. But he is also a social butterfly; he talks with all of his friends and discusses the "functions." He is not serious about academic success, preferring instead to "B.S." his way through and survive on his mediocrity.

Biff will probably graduate, with something close to a C average, in a weak and undesirable major. He will then complain that the job market has dried up and there are no good jobs for Distributed Studies majors. Biff has ended his own future with mediocrity, but he is too lazy and insecure to admit it.

Respect your own time

For you, it is not too late. When you study, make the studying count! Your time is precious, so don't waste it!

I always recommend study breaks, but certainly not every five minutes. When you do take breaks, try to make them last no longer than five minutes, and you will notice that you can remain refreshed and devoted to study, and be more productive too.

If you study with complete devotion, you will find that your study sessions seldom last more than a few hours (mine averaged three hours).

After the studying, socialize! This is the fun part of college! Relax and discuss the meaning of life, or watch old M*A*S*H reruns.

Academic success is your priority, you have contributed to that success, and now you can take it easy for a while. The attitude is all-important.

Types of Classes

As I attended classes in college I discovered that there are in general four types of class:

The required reading class

The required writing class

The project class

The story problems class.

(These types omit such classes as physical education, but you can adapt the suggestions here to those special cases.)

Each of the types requires a different method of study, and over the course of my college years I developed different methods to succeed in each type of class.

The Required Reading Class

Classes in fields such as psychology, history, and management tend to fall into this category. These classes typically require reading of about one chapter per week, usually about 30 pages.

Most of the time lectures in these classes will expand on or draw directly from the reading. The test questions will usually be essay, short answer, or matching, and will invariably come mostly from the reading. Do you get the idea that doing the reading is very important?

Simply reading the chapters is often not enough, however. Most study guides will tell you to read the chapter through before you attend the lecture over that chapter; I am going to let you off the hook and tell you not to.

Skim

Most college students don't read the chapters before lectures anyway, and you might as well not feel guilty; there are other ways to succeed. My method (which works for people with good note-taking habits and just a small amount of dedication) is to simply skim the chapter to be discussed before the first lecture over the chapter.

For example, if you glance at your syllabus and see that "Chapter Six: The Freudian Method" will be discussed next Monday, Wednesday, and Friday, my method requires you to skim chapter six Sunday night.

There is another good reason to skim first: often, before the first lecture over a chapter, even if you read the chapter you will not understand the material. Blame this fact on poor writing or difficult subject matter, but it happens.

A good skim will introduce you to the concepts, and allow you to at least familiarize yourself with the terms in the chapter. That way when the lecture begins with new words and abbreviations, you will know what the instructor is talking about.

Look at pictures

Skimming means you pay attention to summaries, definitions, graphs, pictures, figures, marginal notes, and all of the other fun stuff in the chapter.

Try not to spend more than a minute per page, but don't skim so quickly that you can't recall any of what your eyes saw. After a good skim you should be able to tell someone (without looking) several of the main points of the chapter.

Many text books include a list of objectives or main points at the beginning of each chapter; copy these down onto a sheet of paper after your skim and see if you can at least tell where in the chapter the objective or point is discussed. Isn't skimming easy?

Attend lectures

After the first lecture on a chapter of required reading, read the chapter.

The first lecture will probably not have gone into too much detail, and your skim, together with this first lecture, will help you to learn on your own the points discussed in the reading.

This is a hint: if you learn on your own the correct information, you will be much better off than if you simply let others tell you the concepts and points. This is why your elementary school teachers told you to look up words rather than simply telling you their definitions.

Read thoroughly this time

When you read, pay attention to concepts. For example, in The Freudian Method, why did Freud adopt that method? Did it work? What do people think of the method today? How would you change the method, and why? Ask yourself questions such as these, and answer them from the reading or from your understanding of the reading.

And here is the good part: if you don't understand some concept or objective from the reading, you still have the rest of the week to discuss it with your instructor; instructors love to discuss concepts.

Jot down important points

While you are doing this reading, take notes on the chapter. You can outline the chapter (I liked to do this) or you can simply jot down main ideas and concepts, but the idea behind taking notes on the chapter is *so you don't have to read the entire chapter ever again.*

Again I let you off the hook. Don't plan to reread all of the chapters before a test! This method is somewhat unconventional, but the reasons are simple: after you understand the concepts and ideas presented in a chapter, the rest is just filler material.

Don't waste your valuable time rereading what the author put into a book simply to "fatten" the book up a little! After this first thorough reading you should be able to rely on your notes, and use the text chapter simply as a reference.

This method assumes, as stated before, that you have good note-taking ability. Good note-takers don't simply copy everything out of the book or lecture; they expand on the concepts as well.

If you outline the chapter and after your thorough reading you can discuss intelligently the concepts and objectives of the chapter, then you need not reread the chapter; just study your notes!

Know your instructor

A word of caution, however: find out if your instructor in this required reading class is a stickler for details like dates and names. When you find instructors who like details as well as concepts don't change the study method; simply include the details in your notes. The chances are good that these instructors will refer to the details in their lectures anyway.

After the last lecture over a given chapter, review your lecture notes and your notes or outline from the text. The two should be very familiar to you and should also be very similar, unless your instructor tends to ramble.

Review your notes

Spend about 20 minutes looking over the concepts, and pay special attention to any statements that appear to be contradictory. Many instructors make mistakes, or actually do not believe what is written in the text; ask your instructor for clarification on any facts or concepts that are unclear to you.

A few days before a test in a required reading class, pull out those notes (both sets) and refresh yourself with the concepts and facts.

Review until all of the concepts make sense to you (even if you don't agree with them!) If you know you have a hard time remembering such details, make some flashcards! If something still isn't clear, call or visit with your instructor; they love to talk!

If you know you have trouble remembering everything you can do several things: selectively eliminate portions of your notes you think will not be on the test (Warning: very dangerous), or ask your instructor what will be covered on the test, or simply begin to study earlier.

Question yourself

Perhaps you could review every chapter's notes every week; by test-time you would have little trouble remembering, for the material would be well-ingrained in your mind.

If you have taken good lecture notes, thoroughly read the chapters and taken notes on them, and reviewed the material to gain understanding of the objectives and concepts, the required reading test should be pretty easy.

Take the test

Those questions you asked yourself while you thoroughly read the chapter will probably appear in some form on the test, and short answer/fill in the blank questions will look like lines directly from your notes.

Essay questions will be easy because you have a good understanding of the concepts, and you know how to express the concepts in your own words—that's what you did when you took notes from the text book.

The worst part about required reading classes and tests is not knowing what the instructor thinks is important enough to ask test questions about. If your instructor chooses not to tell you specifically what you are to know for the test (concepts and facts) then you must simply be more diligent and thorough in preparing for the first test or two. After one or two tests you will be able to make a better estimate of what your instructor thinks is important; adapt your study habits accordingly.

Don't panic the night before the first test and spend half the night "cramming" and losing sleep; if you took good notes, reviewed and understood concepts, and asked questions when you didn't understand, you will do well.

And I assure you, there will be other tests; your success in life does not depend on the first test!

The Required Writing Class

The bulk of the grade in required writing classes comes from papers and writing assignments.

The assignments could be creative writing, interpretation, or essays on a given subject. Required writing classes include literature courses, English composition, and communications courses.

You know how to read and write; otherwise you wouldn't be planning to attend college and you wouldn't understand this sentence. This book is not a primer for English, and is not concerned with your current writing skill level.

You know how well you can write, and our goal is to help you succeed using your skill and the knowledge imparted in this book. Therefore, take an honest look at your writing ability.

Ask a critic

Ask an English teacher in high school whether or not your writing will stand up to the scrutiny of college professors. And take any suggestions your high school English teacher offers regarding honing your personal writing skills.

Show what you know

Since you possess the skills, all that is left is to prove it to the college instructors. Writing assignments mean you will be required to convey your thoughts about a particular subject in the concise and restrictive manner of the written word. Assignments in required writing classes may look something like this:

> *"Discuss the historical significance of the Boston Tea Party; pay special attention to the British Perspective, as explained in your text. Include quotes from your text, if you wish, but do not merely summarize; instead comment on the significance of such material."*
>
> *Four pages, plus title page and bib.*
>
> *Typed, double spaced*
>
> *Due date: Monday*

Make yourself clear

The actual assignment in most of the required writing classes (especially the Freshman Comp and English classes) is: *Write something that makes sense!* Keep this little pearl of wisdom in mind when you struggle to put words on paper.

Instructors are interested in seeing that you have at least a partial understanding of the concepts relating to the assigned subject; more importantly, they are interested in seeing that you can convey this understanding to them.

In simpler terms, how you write (mechanics, grammar, sentence and paragraph structure) is as important as the things you write about.

Beverly Parks Faaborg and Tony Faaborg

Clarify the assignment

How do you write to please the instructor and meet the assigned requirements? Find out what the instructor wants!!

Most instructors have some expectation of what constitutes a good paper; unfortunately, most instructors do not get very specific when it comes to assigning papers.

Take the Boston Tea Party paper assignment, for example. You could easily write a small book about the historical significance of the so-called Boston Tea Party! The first step is to narrow the topic.

The instructor has already hinted that a British perspective is necessary, and has indicated that you are to glean information from the text; these two facts narrow the topic considerably, but not quite enough.

Pick a topic

Now you must be resourceful. Consider the assignment, and try to think of three different "narrow topics" your paper could discuss, all worthy of at least the assigned four pages of writing. Then present these ideas to your instructor, and ask which of the three narrow topics is the most promising, and whether the topic is narrow enough.

Your instructor will most likely be very willing to help you pick and narrow a subject, for he or she will, after all, be reading and grading the final work.

Now that you have a workable and acceptable topic, follow your writing method (the one that worked in high school, updated and practiced for college) and begin to carry out the assignment.

Write a rough draft

After you have finished some sort of rough draft, put the paper aside for awhile and consider the initial assignment and any handouts the instructor may have distributed. Are you still meeting the requirements? Does the instructor (or college!) have any expectations regarding grammar, spelling, punctuation, and mechanics? Now is the time to pay attention to such things, or you will surely pay the price later!

Follow accepted form

Many colleges distribute guidelines for such things as footnotes, bibliographies, quotations, and word usage, to be used when completing writing assignments in any college class.

The reason for such guidelines and rules is so that different instructors can grade papers uniformly, and pay more attention to the subject matter of the paper (yes, subject matter is still important).

Don't handicap yourself! Find out whether your school has such guidelines and rules regarding writing assignments, and follow them to the letter!

Polish the final draft

You have heard this a million times, but don't wait until the last minute to start your papers. You are organized well enough that you know in advance when writing assignments are due, and you know how much time you personally will have to devote to accomplish a good paper.

Instructors can tell when papers have been hurriedly finished, and (believe me) tend to grade such papers more harshly! Reward your organization skills and preparation with good grades!

The Project Class

Project classes such as Architecture, Design, and Radio and Television Broadcasting require you to submit assigned projects (drawings, models, research, productions, and so forth) for grades. Often the projects will account for the majority, or even the entirety, of the course grade.

I consider project classes to be a mixed blessing. On one hand, instructors usually assign between one and five projects in a given course over the entire semester, and you know weeks in advance when the project will be due.

On the other hand, I (and most college students) tend to put off doing assignments, and that means rushing the project to completion the night before it is due.

You can tell which students on campus are taking project classes. They are the ones who seldom sleep, who skip classes between one and five times per semester when projects are coming due.

Why do students subject themselves to the torture of "all-nighters" and frantic work and skipping classes when these same students knew two weeks in advance that the project they are ruining their health over would come due on the specified date?

Many students simply do not grasp that projects assigned two weeks in advance will require more than one night's time to accomplish in a satisfactory form. Take a clue from the amount of time given to complete a project; two weeks, for example. Would you expect that an instructor assigning a two-week project believes it can be completed in one night?

Others use the rationale that they work better or become "inspired" under pressure. Baloney. The truth is they simply become desperate, and the ideas and work they put into the project when "pressured" are no better than ideas they would have had at any other time during the two weeks, only less developed and more haphazard.

So how do you avoid the procrastination temptation and allow yourself to sleep well at night? Once again, the answer is organization and a little persistence.

Start planning now

When you receive the assignment write weekly reminders ahead of time to yourself in your notebook; this way, you will not "forget" that the assignment exists.

In addition, on the very first night after the instructor assigns the project, take stock of your position. Can you complete the project with available materials? Do you have the required literature? Do you have a thorough description of project requirements, either in your notes or from an assignment sheet?

Get your supplies now

Spend about 15 minutes looking over the project requirements, and ask yourself if you have everything you need to finish the project if you started right now. If you honestly do not, then make a shopping list.

Prepare for the project by purchasing any supplies and obtaining reading material.

If you are not completely sure of the requirements and expectations of the project, ask your instructor within the next 24 hours! Don't procrastinate!

Take one step at a time

Next, try to separate the project into several component parts, each to be completed before the project is finished. As an example, say you have three weeks to complete a wood and paper model of a building of your own design.

After obtaining all of the necessary materials and a complete list of requirements, you are ready to dive in and build the model, right? Wrong.

Where do you start? A project such as this (especially if it is the first of several such projects) can look very intimidating in its whole form. Therefore, break it off into bite-size chunks!

In our example, you will have to draw some kind of floorplan, as well as several views of the structure. You will also have to fabricate a frame and possibly some kind of foundation. Next come the walls, and any furnishings in accordance with the project requirements.

If you outline (on paper) the steps to be followed in completing this project you may be surprised at how logically you can think and plan, and at how easy each individual step actually is. Now you are ready to dive in.

Do it now

Here is where students either sink or swim. You have planned your project, you have started early, and you know (from relying on your notebook) when the project is due.

Now do it! At any cost do not put off this project! Procrastinating makes worthless all of the effort you expend to prepare and organize.

Procrastinating also starts you down the road to all-nighters and academic mediocrity instead of excellence. You and your grades are worth more than a brand of "mediocrity."

Start with a couple of hours per night on this project; you will quickly find out just how long the project will take, and you can plan accordingly. And, with just a little bit of discipline and good work, you will be on your way to completing a project you can be proud of.

The Story Problems Class

Do you remember those story problems in elementary and high school math classes?

Train A traveling due west at 60 miles per hour (mph) overtakes train B traveling due west at 48 mph.

If train B left the station 1.5 hours earlier than train A, how long did it take train A to overtake train B?

Doesn't it ever end?

Did you think graduation from high school meant never having to face another story problem? Think again!

If you choose to major in a "pure" science such as physics, chemistry, or math, or in an "applied" science such as engineering, you will be faced with story problems exclusively.

However, you will find story problems of other sorts in economics, psychology, anthropology, home economics, education, and a host of other classes.

The simple fact is that life is a story problem, and there is no better way to practice for life outside of college than to practice story problems in college. And instructors love torture, too.

When you saw the preceding story problem, how did you react? Did you have flashbacks of high school, panic, and begin throwing things? Of course you are not required to solve this one (the answer is six hours), but try to solve it anyway, and arrive at the correct answer.

In math problems especially, but true in all story problems classes, you can develop a system for solving those story problems that will lead you to crystal-clear understanding of the subject matter and praise and admiration from your instructors and classmates (OK, that may be stretching the imagination a bit).

Start with the facts

When confronted with any story problem, write on a clean sheet of paper what is given in the problem.

In the preceding example you know the two trains' respective speeds, and you know how long the second train waited after the first train left.

You also know they travel in exactly the same direction, so you will not need trigonometry.

I find it helpful to draw some sort of diagram. This practice is more appropriate for math and physics problems, but it can find use in other classes too.

What is the question?

Next, write down what you are expected to discover. In the preceding example we were asked to find how long the second train had to travel before overtaking the first train. You will never do well at a story problem if you do not know what you are looking for!

Have I done this before?

Now use some common sense. College textbooks (especially math books) follow a long-standing procedure: introduce a concept, provide exercises over that concept, provide exercises over that concept and other previously learned concepts, introduce a new concept, and so on.

Is this a story problem exercising your newly gained knowledge or past experience? Are there sections of your text devoted to similar problems? What concepts are exercised in the story problem?

Often you will be able to find example problems very similar to the assigned story problems. Don't hesitate to work these example problems (and arrive at the same solution) before attempting assigned story problems.

Many text books include an "Answers to selected exercises" section anyway, so you will not be cheating if you work already knowing the answer. In college the process is as important as the answer; sometimes learning the process is actually the real goal.

You should, by the time you have worked a few problems, know how the solution fits, and know why it fits, and have a decent working knowledge of the concepts involved in the solution. In college, the question is not *what* (as in high school) so much as *why*.

Armed with the concepts, the given information, and the expectations, all neatly presented (by you or the book), you should be able to proceed to solve the problem.

Give me a hint

Always be on the lookout for hints! For example, if there is seemingly not enough information, you will probably have to solve for this information first, then proceed with the problem solution. Or, you might not need the information anyway!

This type of problem can be especially aggravating at first, but stick with the concepts and they will lead you home every time. Also, look at the "given" material.

Rarely in college texts will the authors give you much extraneous or unneeded information. Therefore you can take a hint from the information given.

In physics this practice is known as "plug and chug": given a concept such as $E=mc^2$ or $F=ma$ or $PV=nRT$, and given all but one of the variables in the concept, simply insert (plug) the known material and solve (chug) the equation for the unknown variable.

However, watch out!! Authors and instructors know this practice well. If you "plug and chug" without knowledge and understanding of the concepts, you will be in trouble when the author or instructor decides to trick you! (And they do like to do it once in a while.)

Think positive

Don't roll over and die in story problems classes if you don't like story problems. Attack them! Look at story problems this way: authors can fit fewer of them on a page, and you will probably have fewer of them assigned!

In a nutshell...

Follow "the system": Write down what is given, Write down what is unknown, look for concepts to apply, look for hints and examples, and solve the problem. Simple, eh?

Oh, oh! Test time!

Many students can solve the homework story problems, and then do poorly on story-problem tests. Why does this happen? One answer is students have relatively unlimited time in which to complete homework assignments. You can devote hours, if needed, to one problem.

Tests are different. You must work quickly and accurately on story-problem tests; otherwise, you will never finish the test! So how can you work quickly on the tests? Practice!

One good thing (in a sadistic sort of way) is you will have access to an overabundance of exercises and story problems related to the material! Solve every related problem you can get your hands on, and before long, you will discover that you can solve even the difficult problems quickly.

Believe me, it feels good to be the first one to finish a test in a course you thought you would surely fail, and receive one of the highest grades in the class! The secret is "the system": either the one illustrated here or one you develop on your own.

Just remember...

The most important advice to be given regarding a Story Problems class is learn the concepts; "plug and chug" when you are able, and use ingenuity whenever you can. That's the essence of college!

You Have the Brains

No college student fails because of low I.Q. If you have made it through high school and have been admitted to State U, then there is only one reason to fail—your own study habits!

If you run into academic difficulties, take advantage of the counseling center, professor conferences, help-sessions, and tutors.

You will succeed at college if you seek help if needed, take charge of your time, and say no to distractions.

Chapter 7
Changing Mascots
in the Middle
of the Game
(Switching majors and colleges)

Deciding what you want to do with your life is pretty heady stuff. Do other people seem to "have it all together" and be less doubtful than you? Do not be misled! Lots and lots of people change their minds about fields of study and colleges to attend.

First majors are temporary

While we are on the topic of changing majors, let's discuss that all-important selection of your *first* major. It's the first major because, quite honestly, you probably won't graduate with the college major you select in high school or during your first year of college.

To prove this to yourself, find information on high school graduates from your school two years ago. Find out what they planned to do after high school, and what they are actually doing now. Most will probably have said that they will attend some college and major in some prestigious degree program such as architecture, medicine, engineering, or law.

Now compare these plans with what actually happened. You will find some not even in school anymore! And others will have changed their major at least once in their first two years of college.

Pick a major, any major

You should not struggle too much to think up a major for yourself during your high school years. When you have been a high school senior for a while and people start bugging you about your college plans, select the first major that pops into your head and tell people that major is the one you have selected. Most people simply want an answer, any answer. Don't lose sleep because you don't have a set-in-stone plan for the next four years of your life. The next four years will be full of surprises anyway!

Look within and without

Eventually, though perhaps not until two years after college entrance, you will have to declare a major. This official declaration can wait, however. The best thing you can do toward actually selecting a major while still in high school is to honestly look at your performance and abilities in various subjects.

You will probably have very definite strengths and favorite subjects, and quite logically you should consider emphasizing these strengths and subjects in your college education.

Talk to your school guidance counselor about the various "hot" fields (the careers that are in demand right now or that earn people a lot of money) and see if you can match your strengths and favorite subjects to one or more of these career fields.

When you have found one or several likely career fields, make your goal during your first year of college to simply learn more about these careers, and how you would be required to prepare for them. Then, with the help of a college academic advisor, select courses your freshman year that will do two things:

1. Begin your training for an appropriate degree in your chosen career fields, and

2. Allow you to learn more about what people do in your chosen career fields.

If you do some if this type of planning—discover your own strengths and preferences, investigate the career options, and select appropriate college courses—you will probably have little need for the rest of this chapter! You will be well on your way toward a rewarding career; all that is left is the grades.

Keep your options open

At this time I suggest that you do your best your freshman year to take flexible courses. While you are doing your best to learn about and train for your chosen career field, you can also guard against having to spend more time and money in school than is necessary by selecting courses that are general enough to apply to a variety of majors.

For example, let's say that your selected major requires you to take a two-credit public speaking class. On the other hand, other majors (ones that also interest you) require a three-credit public speaking class that contains the two-credit class plus a section on interpersonal communication. Don't burn your bridges!

If you think that there is any chance that you will change majors in the future, seriously consider taking the more flexible classes. In this example you should probably take the three-credit public speaking class; most majors will accept more than the minimum curriculum, but no major accepts less than the minimum.

I repeat: during your freshman year of college, when you are not completely sure of your future, don't burn your bridges.

Why quit?

Why do students change majors? Worse yet, why do people drop out of school? The answers are numerous, but there are basic reasons, and I guarantee you will hear them or use them yourself! Some basic reasons follow:

1. I don't like the subject matter. Students sometimes think that because certain classes are boring or irrelevant that the major in general is not fun or will be unrewarding. Just remember that one class does not a degree make.

2. I don't understand the material. This is usually an excuse used after people realize that they are so far behind (because they didn't study) there is no hope of catching up. So they change majors in an effort to save face.

3. I'm too dumb. Many students fear failure, but you have to realize that if you are to succeed, you must take risks. I know several people who will testify that virtually anyone can succeed in virtually any major, provided they study, work at success, and simply believe in themselves.

4. I don't want to do _____ for the rest of my life.

Many students make the mistake of thinking that career work in a certain field will be exactly like what they do in the classroom. Not true! Most college classes are rather theoretical, with several case studies and applications of knowledge sprinkled in once in a while. Don't make the mistake of thinking that you will work with weird theories, story problems, and pop quizzes on the job!

In college you do not learn a career; you instead learn ideas and obtain "tools" to help you succeed in a given career.

This major is just *not* me

You may have done your best planning, but after taking classes for a while you realize that the major you initially selected before college is not compatible with you now. What can you do? Is there any hope of graduating? Of course there is hope of graduating with some degree, but you should seriously consider the various alternatives you have available to you.

First, consider why you wish to change majors. No one but you can say whether your reasons are legitimate and point to change, so you should be honest with yourself. Is whatever problem you have temporary? Have you given the present major a fair chance? What is the worst that can happen if you don't change majors now?

Second, investigate alternatives to staying in your present situation. You may be able to simply alter your emphasis within your major, and that would solve the problem. In secondary education, for example, you could emphasize a math/computers curriculum rather than history; changing emphasis is serious, but is not usually as complicated as changing majors outright. Other alternatives include altering your degree program (with the consent of your academic advisor) within your present major, or abandoning the major entirely.

Know the consequences

Once you have found several alternatives, determine the consequences of selecting a given alternative. Changing majors completely usually results in the following consequences:

1. Increased time requirement. You will probably have to add at least one semester (or perhaps summer school) because not all of your credits for one major will be usable in the new major. This is an important consequence to consider when picking a major.

2. Have to pay more money. Increased time requirement implies you will have to pay more money into the system, but there are other money requirements too. For example, architecture students continually invest in supplies for their major.

3. Unnecessary class work. This is more psychological, but some majors have required classes or classes very similar to classes in other majors. If you change majors you will probably have to attend

the required classes, and you may find yourself in classes where you experience *deja vu* all the time because you have already learned much of the material.

The new major

After you have done a lot of thinking, and have discovered a new major suitable to your needs and abilities, go to your academic advisor and present the idea. This visit should be no surprise to your advisor, since you should have been working on your plans already.

Your advisor will have various forms for you to fill out, and will be able to tell you exactly what you need to do to change majors and have the college recognize your intentions. Follow all instructions to the letter, and then follow up with administrative people in both your new and your old major, to make sure that your changes are official and that you haven't missed some important piece of information.

Once you have settled into your new major, you will have some sense of let-down or discouragement, and of course these feelings are normal. Don't feel that you have failed. You have actually done something courageous: you have taken control of your life and you have made a decision that many college students fear to make.

While your new major will take time to get used to, regard it as a challenge; put your efforts into success and you will be rewarded.

When State U eliminates your major

This will actually happen to some students at the college you attend. Bigger colleges and universities always revise their course and curriculum offerings, and in the process, de-emphasize or even eliminate certain majors.

Don't worry if you are planning on a curriculum on which the college was founded (such as engineering at a polytechnic university) and don't worry if you are planning to attend a smaller college. Most of the time colleges don't cut their "bread and butter" programs.

Changing schools

However, you still may find yourself in the situation of having to (or simply desiring to) change colleges. If the first school eliminates your degree program, obviously that is a good reason to change schools (or at least change majors), but you may find another reason to change schools. For example, if you decide to change emphasis in your major, or if you wish to change majors, you may find that your present school doesn't offer the new program you wish. Now it's decision time.

Before you change schools completely, pretend you are once again a high school senior investigating college for the first time. When you look for a new school use the same criteria that led you to your first college, but add in the appropriate degree or emphasis program you wish to enroll in. If you can find another school that fits your criteria and offers the desired degree or emphasis, then you should by all means investigate the possibility of actually changing institutions.

Once you settle on an institution, contact the new school's admissions office (or work with your present advisor to help you) and find out what you and your present school need to do in order to get you into the new school. Most of the time applying and getting accepted at a new school is as easy (or difficult) as it was the first time around. The difference is you will not be so confused by the process, and you will actually have some college "experience" in the form of credits.

Transferring credits

On the subject of college credits, at some point you will have to obtain a college transcript and have it evaluated at the other institution. The transcript shows, for better or worse, how you fared in classes at your present school, and allows the new school to credit you accordingly.

Transcripts include the course name and the grade you received in the course; advisors at the new school will try to match each course you have taken to a course offered at their institution. For example, I took "College Anatomy and Physiology" at one college and it transferred as "Zoology 153" at the new school; most classes will transfer as something.

Occasionally you will hear a person mention "... my credits didn't transfer," referring to either changing majors or changing institutions. This is wrong. Of course the credits transferred, because the classes are legitimate (recognized as "real" at one institution) and are similar to classes offered at other institutions.

Students actually refer to what degree requirements their credits fulfill. For example, let's say that you took six semesters of college calculus in preparation for an engineering degree. Art history as a major does not require six semesters of calculus. If you change majors to art history, you will not reduce your remaining course requirements by the equivalent of six semesters of calculus! Some of your calculus credits may fit in as a math requirement, others may fit in as elective credits, and some may simply fit in as classes you took for no reason.

This last category is the reason changes of major or college require students to stay in college longer in order to earn a degree. Many people blame the community college when credits "don't transfer." In reality the student failed to plan ahead or else switched fields!

The truth hurts—your credits will transfer, all right, but they may not transfer as anything useful.

Telling your parents

After finding an appropriate institution, talking with admissions and with your advisor, present the plan to your parents. They should be the first to know that you are considering such a move, but now give them the details. Prove to them (and to yourself) that this move will be beneficial to you, and show them the consequences (money, time) of the move.

If you can honestly show that the benefits outweigh the consequences you will probably sell them on the idea. Here is a hint: most parents are more receptive to changes of major or college when good grades are involved. Don't fall back on the previously mentioned excuses, and don't use these changes as a way to escape bad grades; excuses and bad grades will come back to haunt you.

College isn't for me; maybe the Peace Corps...

As much as I love college, and as important as it is in my life, I realize that other people do not share my feelings. Many people elect not to attend college after high school, preferring to make their mark in the work world. Others, unfortunately, attend school for a while only then to discover that college is not for them.

If, sometime down the road, you find yourself questioning the value of college in your life, you must do some serious personal investigation. Why did you attend school in the first place? Are those first reasons still appropriate? Can you find any reason to stay in school?

Many high school students tell their parents and all of their friends "I will be attending State U in the fall, majoring in computer science." For the first two weeks of school they are happy with their first decision. Then the exams start. Suddenly the chosen major doesn't look as inviting. I know some students who simply gave up at this point. They realized that the first major they chose was not one they wanted to pursue, so they simply faded away and eventually dropped out of school.

If you decide that you want to drop out of school, ask yourself why. Then write the various reasons on a piece of paper and read them several times. Do your best to avoid temporary excuses, such as instructors or certain classes, or even a given major. (We have already discussed that you can, and sometimes should, change majors.) Evaluate your potential for success and how hard you have worked to realize your goals of success. Could some of the written-down reasons be eliminated if you simply worked harder? The truth sometimes hurts, but you will have to sacrifice a little to succeed.

Look down the road

Finally, consider the long-term effects of dropping out of school. Sadly, most students who drop out of college never return (whether they say they will or not). In this day and age, college education is required for many jobs. And college is simply a great place to grow personally and socially. Even one completed year of college would put you at a very definite advantage over others; it would prove that you really do have the ability to succeed in school.

If, after all of this soul-searching, you believe that you should no longer continue your college education, contact your parents and tell them why. It may help to tell them your reasoning, and possibly any alternative plans you have developed.

Your parents will obviously be concerned for you, but make sure that they understand that this is a personal decision that doesn't reflect on them in any way. Sometimes (like now) you have to make the important decisions in your life, and you have to be ready to personally accept the consequences.

If you ever do plan to drop out, do you best to remain in school at least for one year. I cannot stress enough that any college experience is good, and one year of school will prepare and qualify you for many jobs that would not be available to you otherwise. If you take a position that doesn't require any college experience, you may still be rewarded for your one year in school—increased pay, and perhaps quicker promotions. If you ever do decide to go back to school, one year of college will usually apply very easily to almost any program you might choose. And who knows? Maybe after one year of school you will realize that you are 25% done with a college degree, and that you can survive another 25%, and so on until that magic day when you realize that you will actually graduate.

Drop out correctly

Officially separating from an institution is not difficult, so don't just "fade away!" Tell your academic advisor of your plans, and make sure that the administration at your school knows when you will be officially "not attending school." Without this official separation you will still be treated as a student, and you may still receive student information, failing grades, and possibly even bills!

Act wisely

A certain amount of change will occur during your college life. You will probably change majors at least once, and you may even change schools or drop out of college altogether. Just remember that if you make the decisions, be ready to accept the consequences. Do your best to investigate alternatives first, and then make the best decision you can make with the information available to you. And especially consider the long-term effects.

College isn't forever, and it isn't supposed to be 100% fun. Change isn't bad and it is "normal." Change will shape your future; control the changes in your life and you will control your own future.

Notes to Parents

Lots of people change majors—sometimes between freshman orientation and registration. You do not need to be overly concerned if you have never heard of the field of study, because chances are that it will change—sometimes between registration and the first week of classes.

Lots of people also fail courses. If you ask around, you will find that the local Spanish teacher failed Spanish, the kid down the block is on "temporary enrollment," and the doctor's daughter is retaking physics.

The family honor does not depend on success in biochemistry. The day will probably come when you get a phone call saying Muffi wants OUT—either out of a class, a major, or out of college altogether.

There are four reactions which can help you help Muffi.

1. Be honest. Ask yourself if it is really that Muffi is ruining her life, or is it that you are disappointed because you always wanted a doctor in the family? Are you simply embarrassed to say OUT LOUD that your daughter is going to make bagels instead?

2. Make suggestions. Sometimes the obvious solutions have not been considered, so ask Muffi if she has given any thought to ...dropping a couple of courses this semester... talking to a senior in that major... going to the counseling center... giving it one more week...

3. Think positive. Rather than put yourself through the agony of worrying about your child being sorry later, try to focus on the

positive. There is hardly any career decision which cannot be reversed later, so maybe in another semester (or year) she will give up beachcombing art and return to robotics.

4. Ask questions. Ask your child and yourself: what is the worst that could happen? Is it that she will fail a course? Have to re-take a class? Need an extra semester? Lose a scholarship? Keep these things in perspective.

On the other hand, there are a couple of "don'ts" for you to consider. Especially, do not be an financial "enabler" who makes it easy for the child to make bad choices.

1. Do not keep pouring money into a black hole. If your child is being a party animal and flunking out, maybe one of the suggestions for financing college in chapter 2 would be better. i.e. have him pay tuition and then you reimburse him for courses he passes.

2. Do not bail him out of messes he has made. There must be unpleasant consequences for his actions or he will never learn responsibility. If he changes majors two or three times and colleges a couple of times, set a time limit on your financial support.

3. Do not provide a comfortable unearned lifestyle. Why should anyone graduate and get a job as long as he can live at college or at home free, with no responsibilities?

Remember that your child is grown up. Be pleased that you are involved and informed in the decisions to switch directions.

Give the same caring support that you expect from your family when you do something big (or dumb!)

Chapter 8
Seriously Speaking
(physical and mental health)

You will notice normal expected changes in your life after you have been away from home for the first time and begin to show your independence. However, college age is a critical time for some heavy things to happen. This is probably the first time you will be really out from under the parental roof and trying to settle on a way of life and value system of your own. Be alert for signs that "something is not quite right."

This chapter is not meant to be a sermon or a lecture in addition to the many your parents have given you. We simply want to alert you to several serious problems that can develop while you attend college; if you do not watch out and are not aware of the signs, you may fall into trouble before you realize it!

Physical Health

Until now Mom has monitored diet, sleep, exercise, medication. You may notice a dramatic change in sleep patterns, exercise, and stress. Although your sleep and rest habits will probably change normally in college, watch for indications of fatigue, attitude changes, lingering illnesses, or behavior changes.

If you suspect something may be wrong, follow your gut feelings and investigate. The student health center can advise, or you can talk to your family doctor. Go home for a weekend and visit with your parents (after all, they do know you pretty well). Talk to your room-mate or friends, and you may find they are feeling the same way or they have indeed noticed something about you.

Above all, do not put off finding help if you think you may need it.

Party pizza and the dreaded green gelatin

You will probably notice that your eating habits are among the first to change when you go off to college. You no longer have someone cooking especially for you; in the dormitories at school the cooks prepare for as many as 2000!

Cafeteria-style eating is actually both a positive and a negative experience; you will be exposed to a variety of foods at a reasonable cost, but you will also be subject to the fattening foods and junk food responsible for a mysterious weight-gain known as the "Freshman Fifteen."

I'm hungry, but... FOOD SERVICE?

Unless you are a culinary wizard when you go to college you will not be able on your own to match the variety offered by the dorm kitchens, dollar for dollar. Cooking for 2000 allows food service directors to offer expensive foods like broccoli and pineapple, or chicken kiev, at a reasonable price to you.

Some people complain that you get tired of the food quickly at food service because they always serve "the same old stuff" or that the food is disgusting and deserves the nicknames attached to the various food products. You must understand that making fun of food service is a tradition passed down from generation to generation, whether the food is good or not. Also, those who complain about the lack of variety usually do not get much variety in their diet in the first place.

A typical meal at Food Service will offer two or three entrees, dessert, fruit, a variety of salad options, a vegetable or two, and various beverages like milk and soft drinks. If a person never eats fruits and vegetables and always avoids the salads, then of course the variety is lost—all that are left are a few entrees!

Eating Food Service food gives people the chance to eat all the recommended portions of the four basic food groups:

Fruits and vegetables

>   4 servings per day

Breads, cereals, and grains

>   4 servings per day

Meat, fish, and protein

>   2 servings per day

Milk and dairy products

>   4 servings per day

I strongly recommend that you try to meet all of the recommended serving amounts for each of the four food groups every day. Your health, attitude, and classroom performance will be better if you do. Many young adults find meeting the amounts a lot easier if they have practiced doing so before leaving for college.

At home I suggest you make a chart and keep track of your intake of the four food groups as well as your intake of sweets and junk food.

Do this for about a week and you will probably notice that you have as many as three times the required amount of meat, for example.

If you mark your chart each time you eat and then review it at bedtime, you might find yourself downing three glasses of tomato juice like my brother Tim did in order to meet the requirement of fruits and vegetables for the day. When you begin to notice a trend in your eating habits you will be able to adjust your food selection habits to maintain the best possible balance of the four food groups.

The "Freshman Fifteen"

Maintaining an intake of all of the recommended portions and servings on a daily basis becomes really expensive for individuals who cook for themselves; for this and other reasons some people simply do not eat right while at school. You probably already know someone who practically lives on Twinkies and soda pop; at college the tendency to live on junk food is almost too much to bear at times. College students tend to get much less exercise than they did while in high school, and this fact adds to any already existing eating problem.

People who succumb to the lure of junk food tend to notice their weight increasing during their freshman year of college; women notice their pants fitting a little too snugly, and men get the "spare tire" around the midsection. Remember: your hips and midsections will go home with you during breaks, and your friends and relatives will then know whether or not you have been eating right! I guarantee that almost nothing is worse than Grandma looking down her glasses at you and peering at your new figure inappreciatively.

Unfortunately the weight you gain (or fail to lose) in college can persist later in life; you owe it to your future self to eat right in college. A simple fact to remember is this: food from the four basic food groups will not cause excessive weight gain! In addition, chances are that you will not feel like hitting the chips and soda after three good meals that satisfy the recommended servings and portions. After the recommended portions and servings of the "good stuff," I enjoyed a dessert or late-night pizza with friends; but I never let the pizza party take the place of the fruits and vegetables!

Don't let yourself down by putting on the "Freshman Fifteen," and make sure you eat well; your health is important in keeping the grades high. What makes college so different is the fact that now you are really out from under your parents' wings and you alone have to care for yourself or seek help.

Your body is *your* responsibility now

At college you will be completely responsible for your own physical health; no longer will Mom or Dad be able to diagnose and determine whether you should visit the doctor—it's up to you! You will also be responsible for your own relaxation and sleep schedule. Relaxation and sleep should be major factors in your college life; if they are not you probably won't make the grade.

Your new doctor won't know you

Do you know when you last had a tetanus shot? That could be a life-or-death question! You should have in your possession an up-to-date immunization and disease record with you at school. (It *is* in that red folder of important stuff which we discussed in chapter one, isn't it??)

In addition, become acquainted with the health center on campus or the community hospital. Personnel there can provide you with information on what to do when you get sick (you will eventually get sick—guaranteed) and how to go about paying for your medical bills.

Also, keep in mind that your teeth should probably see a dentist once in a while, and your eyes may require the services of an optometrist sometime during your schooling.

Your medical situation is a very important area for you and your parents to discuss. Chances are, you are covered or at least mentioned in your parents' medical insurance policy; however, coverage could change when you leave home to go to school. In addition to insurance, talk with your parents about medical matters such as where to send bills, emergency numbers where officials can reach them, and so on.

Rest and Relaxation

Many college students do not know how to relax. They spend hours studying, then fall exhausted into bed, or continue to study the night away, or go out partying.

Your brain does need to rest, and you can do yourself a big favor by finding a hobby or learning to simply do nothing. I do not mean to imply that hobbies or doing nothing should be pursued to the exclusion of sleep or studying; you must assess the proper priorities.

The most successful college students allow time for studying, with several breaks spaced in for variety, and time for tossing the books aside to have some fun.

Study breaks can last anywhere from a few seconds to several minutes, but the goal is to let your brain "cool down" for a time. Studying, sleeping, and breaking will minimize the occurrence of headaches (one of the most crippling of "college diseases") and will allow you to actually enjoy life while making the grades.

Sleep in bed, not in class

One of the three "keys to success" at college given in the chapter on success in the classroom is: go to sleep. Obviously, humans need a certain amount of sleep simply to survive. However, minimum survival sleep will not grant you success in the classroom. This may seem obvious and even trite, but I have seen many college students fail because they think they can stay up all night and then make their classes the next day.

It doesn't work. Sometime in your classes, notice your classmates who obviously didn't get a good night's sleep—they will waggle their heads as they nod off, and occasionally they will drop their books on the floor as they lose muscle control. Is this any way to learn anything in the classroom? It is a lot funnier (and better for the grades) to be wide awake and watching these sleeping clowns than it is to be one of the sleeping clowns.

Instructors sometimes get into the act. One I know has his students leave the room while the hapless sleeper dreams—only to wake up to an empty classroom! Another will go to the sleepy student's desk and slam her fist loudly on the desk—a rude awakening, to be sure.

Besides the spectacle and embarrassment of falling asleep in class there are the precious grades. You cannot pay attention in class if you are asleep, and you know as well as I do that those who sleep through a lecture will probably miss material that will appear on a test. Most instructors take some or all of their test questions from lecture material; therefore, the wide-awake (and present) student will actually hear the answers to test questions before the test! Isn't college easy? All you had to do to get some answers was get a good night's sleep!

Listen to your body

Your physical health is really easy to take care of if you just monitor what your body is trying to tell you and take time to let it rest. College comes at a good time for humans because your body is strongest between ages 18 and about 25. Just don't try to be Super student or Wonder partier!

Depression and suicide

Mental health is just as important to college success as physical health, and is more often ignored until it is too late. I know of several people who had nervous breakdowns or bouts with severe depression due to the stress of college. While some mental problems cannot be prevented, many college-related maladies can be.

There are some predictable stresses for each of the four years: Freshmen naturally worry about fitting in academically and socially; sophomores are being pressured to finish basic course requirements and to declare majors; juniors become legal adults as they turn twenty one; and seniors face interviews and leaving the safety of being a student.

An important part of mental health is relaxation and sleep, but you could encounter several mental disorders, either in yourself or in others, that are more serious.

A whole new world

Many new experiences await the college student, but not all of them are good. The high school star athletes realize they are not tops in their sport at college; the high school "A" student must now deal with less-than-superior grades. The high school valedictorian finds it a new experience to be surrounded by students equal to or above his own ability. Gifted students are often overlooked during their growing-up years by teachers, parents, and counselors and many times are unprepared to meet life's disappointments—because they have not been exposed to failures, competition, and rejection. Getting C's and D's on college work has a devastating effect and F's can be disastrous and even life-threatening.

Breaking point

Young adults attempt suicide for a variety of reasons, but frequently the attempt is simply a cry for help. A person can feel the stress bending them to the breaking point, and no human being should be made to endure such an ordeal. Unfortunately, college students are subjected to this stress regularly, and unless the students develop the coping skills necessary to combat suicidal tendencies and severe depression they are headed for trouble.

Try to prepare for the "learning shock" and hone your study skills besides. Refer to the chapter on success in the classroom in this book, but also remember that the high school counselor can suggest books, films, and resources, and the college student services department can help with tutors, group sessions, and individual helps.

What's the worst that could happen?

When the depressed feelings hit you (usually just before or after a big test!) you should always work to put things in perspective. For example, practice the "What's the worst thing that could happen?" coping strategy:

What's the worst thing that could happen if I fail Freshman Calculus?

> *I'd have to retake it.*
>
> *I'd be out of sequence for my other courses.*
>
> *I'd have to go to summer school.*
>
> *I'd have to go an extra semester.*

The worst things usually don't happen, and even if they do, you can handle it—adjust a bit, talk to parents, counselors, advisors, and so forth, and handle it!

Slow down

Sometimes the pace of college is cause for depression—students wonder if they are smart enough to make the grade and begin to seriously worry when their grades seemingly indicate poor ability. Actually, the required *pace* is often the problem, not the students' perceived lack of ability; some students are unprepared for and unable to meet the demands placed upon them in the classroom.

The solution to this "problem" is simple: take fewer classes and take control of the pace! No one says students must take 20 credit hours per semester and be members of several different clubs and hold down a full-time job; if you feel the pace is quickening, you and your advisor can certainly slow it down. Slowing down your pace may involve possible summer school and probably more semesters, but this cost is minor where your well-being is concerned.

Don't go it alone

College is temporary; the classes begin and end, and the problems come and go; suicide is a permanent solution to a temporary problem! The important message here is that people want you to succeed. (We do, or we wouldn't have written this book!)

If you experience problems in the classroom do not hesitate to talk with the instructor; if you are worried about choosing or changing a major, talk with your academic or career advisor.

I find fault with those who claim you will be "just a number" at a faceless institution where everyone goes about the business of higher learning with machine-like precision.

This myth is usually told by people who are afraid to ask for help. Believe it or not, there are people at every college who are paid to listen to your troubles and help you resolve them; all you have to do is ask. College is serious business, but nothing is worth ruining your health (or worse, ending your life) over.

Homosexuality

Homosexuals and persons confused about their own sexuality have a high suicide rate. College is sometimes a turning point for people who have previously hidden homosexual feelings; these people may actually hate themselves for the feelings, or they may feel isolated from the rest of their home community.

When you leave home you are in a position to meet and associate with gays and can test out any confusing feelings you have for the same sex. You might attend gay support group meetings and then realize that you are not gay at all—or you might start to accept the fact that you may be gay and actually adopt a label—gay, lesbian, bisexual.

Young people in this situation, and their parents, need emotional support, information, and resources.

If you find yourself in college with confusing feelings about your sexuality then do your family a big favor and contact the campus gay support groups, mental health centers, hospital chaplain, clergy, and school counselors, for information.

Cults

Many college students recognize religion as a guiding force they need to stay on track, maintain their focus, or provide the "boost" during the rough exam times. However, some groups prey upon the very college students who need this focus or boost; the cult groups promise to "show the way" but seldom deliver.

The very word "cult" makes parents cringe. They are afraid you will take up with a group or movement that has different religious beliefs and rituals, or follow a leader who claims to be divine. Being away from the family's influence, beliefs, and traditional religious practices as well as being alone and searching can leave you ripe for cult influence.

Cults appeal to basic needs

Cult groups meet human needs and appeal to the social nature of people; namely, we all want to be loved and appreciated. They approach people in transition, the anxious, the confused, the lonely, the stressed, and the undecided. College students are all of these!

Cult members approach at key times of pressures and uncertainty: the first week of classes, finals week, and graduation. Members frequent student vacation spots during breaks. Some cults are even campus organizations that use fronts and appear as study groups or religious meetings; or they have booths, concerts, lectures, offer free meals, make dorm visits, and offer weekend workshops.

Prized recruits are the bright, wealthy, creative young people rather than the have-nots of society. Cult members will appear as friendly, warm, interested-in-you people and often begin their first approach with questions such as "Would you like to help make the world a better place to live?" (Of course you probably would, but what is beneath this seemingly innocent question?) The idealistic student who is seeking his own identity is fertile ground for cults. (Sometimes cults are movements of religious protest; while this type of movement is perfectly legal, sometimes the methods employed are not.)

Some tip-offs

Be concerned if the beliefs are based on one leader's teaching, if they cut off communication with family and friends, if members give earnings to the group, if members or leaders engage in consciousness-altering practices (chanting, recitation of memorized material), or if daily work of members is demeaning. Be concerned if they recruit on street corners or approach as if from out of the blue.

Two specific religious sects (both considered cults) are experiencing an increase in popularity in recent years: Witchcraft and Satanism. Most college students who join the ranks of either group are declaring their independence in a rather unorthodox way; but, just as with cults, students do not realize the potential dangers associated with the groups.

Witchcraft

Witchcraft today seems to be in its purest form an attempt to commune or harmonize with nature and the world. Today's witches practice the ceremonies and mystic rituals of old, but the goal is usually for peace or community. The problems arise when members begin to rely on the ceremonies and rituals for their basic social needs; indeed, most "practicing witches" today treat it as more of a hobby than a way of life.

Satanism

Satanism and its effects can be much more devastating, both to the practitioners and to the victims of some honorific rituals. Satanism, or devil-worship, is on the upswing in the United States, as evidenced by the rising number of crimes committed where satanic ceremonies played a part or were actually the cause of the crime. You may see the symbols of satanism on your campus: the pointing-downward five-pointed star or pentagram, the numbers "666", or ceremonial effects such as the colors red and black or even a sacrificed animal carcass.

Be aware

The whole point of this description is to make you aware that there exist people who do perform the ceremonies, who will try to take you in, and who will hurt more than they help. You owe it to yourself to investigate your options concerning these groups and at all times watch that you do not get caught up in the ruse.

Don't over-react

There do exist harmless communes and religious sects that are non-traditional and have genuine concern for the welfare of their members. Be careful that you don't overreact and make accusations of cultism and brainwashing, but be just as careful to get the whole story from the group before you commit to anything! For example, simple meditation and relaxation techniques can have a calming effect.

Some legitimate religious groups simply use non-conventional religious expressions. "Campus" churches, for example, tend to function more as big youth groups due to the preponderance of young people in their congregations. Young congregations tend not to be bound to traditional forms of worship, and feel good about worshiping in new and non-traditional (yet perfectly acceptable) ways. When "shopping" for a church, keep in mind that usually a campus church of a particular denomination will have a conservative counterpart somewhere in the same town.

Alcohol and Other Drugs

Chemical misuse and abuse

Some campuses make their social reputation as party schools through emphasis on drugs, especially alcohol. Law enforcement officials will tell you that drugs, especially alcohol, are a problem on every major college campus in the country.

This book is not intended to act as a sermon or a lecture on the vices of humans; you may feel you are responsible enough to enjoy a few drinks without harm, but you should know the facts before you put your feelings to the test.

The law

The Law doesn't care if you are a straight-A student with a graduate fellowship in the works; if you break the law you will be held responsible under the law.

Investigate the laws concerning providing alcohol to minors, transporting alcohol, possession of and using drugs, host-liability (aiding, tolerating, or ignoring excessive drinking) for guests who drink and then break the law.

You can easily find the laws; any police officer will tell you, and copies of the Code of the state in which you reside can be found in almost any library. Check out the law, and its penalties, and see if you can live with the consequences of breaking any laws relating to drugs.

Protect your mind

Studying and earning good grades are the most important reasons you should attend college; after all, they are the measures of collegiate success. Drug use can impair your study, and cause you to undergo radical personality changes.

Many heavy-drinking college freshmen figure they can party and still make the grade; the problem here is that few freshmen at all have the ability to succeed in college without devoted study and concentration.

Those who party their way through their first year may be in for a shock when the grade reports come back; they may find that they fooled only themselves. As an example, I knew personally two men who earned straight "F" grades their first semester at school. Both now have 0.00 grade-point averages because they drank their grades away.

Did you know?

Many people are misinformed about the effects of drug use and abuse; for example, did you know these facts?

- Alcohol is absorbed directly into the bloodstream, unlike food which is digested slowly.

- The effects of alcohol can be intensified by using along with medicines.

- Carbonated sodas added to alcohol cause it to be absorbed faster.

- Coffee, cold showers, and so forth don't affect the alcohol level or cause it to be burned off faster.

Get out of there

Hanging out with people who "use" is asking for trouble. Sometimes it's beyond your control if you are paired up with a roommate or a group at school who wants to party rather than to graduate. You might need to remove yourself from an unhealthy environment; ask housing officials, such as the head resident or resident assistant, to help with changing roommates or with moving to another dorm.

Practice "no"

To resist the pressures to drink or do drugs you need "refusal skills." Practice or role-play situations you might encounter. You may want to become comfortable with naming the kind of risk involved: "That's possession of a controlled substance!" Or you can suggest alternatives: "Let's go to the football game instead," Or you can leave the situation but keep the door open to being friends: "I'll catch you tomorrow at the gym."

You can do it

If your self esteem is high, your refusal skills are strong, and you have the facts about chemical use and abuse, then you are probably in good shape. Local rehabilitation agencies can help if you want informative brochures, support groups, or education and prevention materials.

Campus Violence

When a person decides to ingest drugs and alcohol the only body affected physically is his or her own. However, crimes such as assault and rape violate the rights and privacy of others. The sobering statistics point to increased violence on campus, and the sad fact is that you must be prepared to prevent or cope with violent crime.

Use your head

Common sense goes a long way in helping to avoid being mugged, robbed, or raped. Naturally, traveling in groups is better than being alone in dark isolated areas. Carry a police whistle. Do simple things such as keeping your room door and car doors locked, and telling people where you are going and when you will return. Many thieves know that people leave their doors unlocked when they shower. Don't leave your door unlocked and return to find your valuables stolen from an open room!

Hate crimes

Hate crimes are simply acts of violence, or actions already determined to be against the law. Campus communities and other cities in the United States are moving to make any degrading action motivated by hate against the law and punishable under the law. If you feel you have been victimized by a hate crime, whether the specific action is against the law or not, contact the campus security force or the police. Reporting crimes of this nature is the first step toward their elimination.

Just be careful

Don't become suspicious of everyone or afraid to venture out, but be cautious and do what you can to prevent anything happening to you. If you are the victim of any kind of wrongdoing, report it immediately. You can do your part to prevent campus crime and to fight it.

Crisis Services

Inform yourself and plan ahead so you know where to turn for routine help and in time of crisis.

Rather than viewing the campus as sprawling acres of thousands of impersonal people, try to break it down into support systems. The college catalog or handbook lists specific resources.

Peers: roommates, dorm advisors, officers, resident assistants, members of special interest groups, clubs, tutors, peer helpers

Faculty: instructors, advisors, sponsors of clubs, organizations

Services: health center, counseling and student services (academic and personal), religious centers, personnel, parent help lines, support groups, student affairs office, minority affairs, university judiciary

Community resources: law enforcement, mental health centers, hospitals, doctors, library, churches, school counselors, organizations—"sister" groups of organizations you belong to back home—scouts, brotherhoods, sisterhoods, fraternal groups, service groups

You deserve the best

This chapter has highlighted several areas of concern to college students. Your health, both mental and physical, is one of the most important factors determining success in school.

The message of this chapter can be reduced to a simple plea: if you suspect in the least that something might be wrong, seek help. Do not feel like you are weak to do so, and do not feel like there is a reward for those who succeed without any help from others. College personnel and health specialists are paid to help you succeed. You deserve their help, and you deserve to succeed!

Notes to Parents

Be positive

During college years, we parents can be positive, concerned, and supportive as we let the young person know there is nothing "wrong or weird" about him and that he is as smart as the next person. Kids who know they are loved unconditionally—with no strings attached seem less likely to get into trouble. Help your child contact and become acquainted with campus groups such as religious groups or special interest groups so he feels a sense of belonging.

Once in awhile your child will call home distraught. After you hang up, you will not sleep a wink and will struggle with handling the problem. What you will find out later is that immediately after you hung up, he talked with a couple of people, solved the problem, went merrily on his way, out for pizza or whatever. That is why the number of gray hairs is figured by multiplying the number of college kid years by the number of offspring you have.

Be honest

Parent example and attitudes toward chemical use is a factor in the child's decisions. We might ask ourselves if he has grown up seeing us medicating for pain and stress, or "needing a smoke or drink". Now is a good time to admit that our own attitudes and actions have been undesirable and let the child know that we haven't acted responsibly ourselves and that as of right now, we're turning over a new leaf.

Be alert

There are some danger signals to be concerned about. If you see these things happening, or if you suspect your college student is dangerous to self or others, get help immediately! Be concerned if he:

        becomes quiet, fatigued, withdrawn
        behaves inappropriately
        skips classes
        has big change in sleeping or eating habits
        seems bored, restless,
        can't concentrate
        exhibits feelings of anger, despair, loneliness, helplessness
        abuses alcohol or other drugs
        becomes violent, over-emotional, rebellious
        puts affairs in order
        neglects appearance
        shows radical personality change
        expresses suicidal thoughts, even jokingly
        has psychosomatic complaints
        seems preoccupied with themes of death
        upset about break-up with boyfriend or girlfriend
        takes dangerous risks

If you have no idea who to contact, consider these as places to call to ask what to do or who to call to get help for your child:

        a national suicide hot line
        a hospital in the college town
        dorm personnel (resident assistant, advisor—
                see the college parent handbook)
        campus counseling center emergency phone
        a member of the clergy in the college town

Suicide scares

When talking to your child during times of extreme stress, try to be calm but do express your concern and care. Listen without judging. You must attend to the immediate concern which is saving a life; all other things which need to be discussed and decided can wait.

Remember: if he completes a suicide attempt, there will be no second chance. You can offer phone numbers and helps to your child, but you also should call for help. If in doubt, err on the safe side!

Let him grow

Kids who have been allowed to feel the pain of their own irresponsible decisions without parents bailing them out or protecting them from consequences are probably mature and responsible by the time they get to college.

However, don't become guilt-ridden if your adult child uses his free will and goes against your family beliefs and values. You did the best you knew how but now he is responsible for his actions and their consequences. Rather than be embarrassed, remember there's just so much parents can do. We can teach, guide, be available, show our love, pray, and hope. The rest is up to the young person.

The family name and honor do not depend on whether or not he passes psychology, or even if he drops out of college. Don't put undue pressure on your child. However, if he is simply enjoying life and playing and partying, offer to send him to a resort instead of college—it's cheaper.

Chapter 9
Hey, Mom,
Remember Me?
(communicating with the home front)

This is actually an embarrassing and guilt-ridden chapter; the plain truth is most college kids (including me) don't communicate with the home front as often as parents would like them to. Because this

disease is so widespread college students have become good at finding reasons not to write or call. The obvious first choice is "I've been
studying too much because _____ (insert reason: big exam, project
due, way behind and have to catch up)." The problem is you won't
fool anyone into thinking you study 24 hours per day and have
absolutely no time to do anything else!

Not communicating is bad because parents automatically assume the
worst—that you have been hit by a bus and are now lying in a ditch
desperately trying to get a message to them as your life's blood drips
away. Save yourself this guilt trip (you will have to face the music
eventually) and communicate!

Don't be a stranger

Before you leave your parents for your first year in college devise a
scheme to keep the communication lines open and to keep you from
getting the guilt treatment. Your parents will probably have some
minimum expectations of you (like how often you will write or call)
so work those into your scheme too. Something as simple as calling
or writing once a week (plus emergencies) may very well keep your
parents happy the entire time you are in school.

Ma Belle or Uncle Samuel

When you are devising this scheme decide what combination of calling and writing you will do. We won't pretend that you don't know the
advantages and disadvantages of one or the other, but there are three
points to consider from the college perspective.

Point number one: Budget. You will probably be operating on
a very tight budget for a few years. How big a phone bill can you or
your parents afford? Your parents might say it's your choice whether
to write or to call since it's your money; it takes a lot of letters to
equal the price of a typical phone call! Also consider that letters can
be read at the recipient's leisure.

Point number two: Timing. College hours are sometimes very
different from home hours. You will regularly find yourself up at 11
p.m., midnight, and beyond; your parents may not appreciate late-
night phone calls. On the other hand, if you can agree on designated

phone times (Saturdays are good; low rates all day) then the timing problem is solved. If your parents say they will almost always be home Tuesday at suppertime or Sunday noon, try to call then.

Your parents will probably have a hard time catching you in your dorm room if they call, so it will usually be better for you to call home. Parents may try to call you at all hours and may become worried when they don't get an answer at midnight or at six in the morning. Answering machines are quite handy and your parents may develop a loving, caring relationship with yours over time.

Point number three: Speed. If you find out Monday that you need a copy of your birth certificate Thursday (Why isn't it in your Important Stuff folder?!) don't take the chance of writing a letter and hoping the return mail will arrive in time! Of course, planning way ahead may solve some of your speed problems. Plan ahead if writing is your chosen method of communicating; otherwise you will find yourself paying for phone calls when Sunday rolls around and you haven't written. Planning ahead means having envelopes, stamps, or postcards on hand.

Address several envelopes in advance so you can grab one as you rush to class. In an emergency, simply dash a quick note on a postcard; parents will count that as a letter for the week.

There's nothing to write about!

Don't use "I can't write well!" as an excuse for not writing. We're talking about your parents—they will love your writing no matter what or how you write. And this is a great time to practice letter-writing; writing letters is an art that can win you jobs, friends, and even money (scholarships, for example).

Parents want to hear the basics; tell them the stuff they normally find out each day when you are home all of the time. How are classes? How is your health? Is anything newsworthy happening at school? Are there any new aspects of you they might want to know about (if you have recently shaved your head you may want to break the news to them)?

Write about the fun things too: parties, games, the new boyfriend or girlfriend. Parents know these activities go on at college; hiding from them what you do with your free time will only make them wonder what's wrong with you or what you are doing and why you haven't told them.

Remember, parents always assume the worst if they aren't told differently.

A mannerly and thoughtful thing to do is to inform your parents about news and happenings before an outsider does. Think how parents feel when a neighbor says "I sure enjoyed talking to your daughter in Tahoe last week." Whether you want it to or not, news does get back home!

If you really want to make your parents melt then go beyond the basics and tell them something about you and them. For example, almost every week you will find something your parents did to make your life a little more comfortable. They probably can't do it in the same way now, so tell them you miss it! Don't worry about flowery speech; pretend you are talking, and just write the words that come out.

Red letter days

Always, always, always remember and be on time with remembrances. A card or phone call is sufficient for birthdays, Mother's Day, and Father's Day. You need just enough of a remembrance for Dad to toss into conversations, "Yeah, when my son called on Father's Day, he remarked...." Or, "Can you believe that my daughter sent this weird card for my birthday??!"

Videos and you

A novel and even fashionable way to show people back home what your new life is really like is to video tape "A Day in My Life at School." Borrow or rent a video camera and shoot at least an hour of scenes around campus, in your room, and with your friends. Have a friend get some shots of you! Include evidence of you studying and attending classes, of course. Each year add onto the tape and at the end of your four years you will have a keepsake from college.

To forward or not to forward

A final note on being no stranger: if you belong to any clubs or mail-order companies, or you have magazine subscriptions, and you want to receive mail at school, tell the companies around six weeks in advance what your new address will be. This applies every time you change your address at school, too. It's amazing how much mail goes to your home address after you leave.

Your parents can forward first class mail, but together decide what to do with magazines, junk mail, and tape club arrivals. Do you want your parents to open certain things and see if they need attention immediately, or should they pay to forward it? Can they pile junk mail up until the your next trip home? You may enjoy receiving all of that junk mail, but your parents may not enjoy saving your "Cheese of the Month" promotional advertisements.

Having stuff sent from home

Letters and phone calls work well for exchanging news and information, but what do you do when you have to ship something bulky like a sweater or something valuable like $500 cash? Consider also that this may or may not be an urgent delivery; is speed important?

U.S. mail

The U.S. Postal Service has perhaps the greatest variety of ways to ship goods; however, look around to compare methods so that you can get the service your job requires at the least cost.

As an example, let's say that you lost your copy of your birth certificate again and you need it in order to take a job tomorrow. Can you count on regular mail to get a copy from your parents to you in time? Perhaps not. Will Overnight Delivery such as special U.S. Postal Service delivery or Federal Express solve your problem? Surprisingly enough, perhaps not! Even the "overnight delivery" places can't always guarantee overnight delivery!

Don't just assume you can mail anything anywhere. Some shipping companies have rather strict requirements on size, weight, and packaging. Before you have to ship, call around to various shipping companies, including the U.S. Postal Service, and check these requirements as well as the costs. You could save big money with a few phone calls.

Moving money

What if you must send a large amount of money to your parents (it sounds crazy and backwards, but it may happen someday)? You probably know better than to send cash through the mail, but what other means are available to you?

Western Union would work. If your parents need the money tonight then you will probably have to use the Western Union wire service. Although this service is comparatively expensive, it is one of the fastest. To find out about the availability of Western Union look in you telephone book white pages under "Western Union." There will probably be a toll-free nation-wide listing as well as a local Western Union terminal location. Give the national number a call or go to the local terminal for information.

FAX

How about sending a copy by FAX (facsimile transmitted by telephone)? If you and your parents can each gain access to a FAX machine your problem may be solved—you could get your copy of important papers in five minutes or less!

Avoid the guilt trip

You need to keep in touch with the home front. It might seem like your parents are trying to control your life from a distance, but the simple fact is that they are interested in you and love you! We never outgrow our need for family support. Witness the fact that *your* parents keep in touch with *their* parents.

Notes to Parents

This business of keeping in touch can get a bit sticky. You will hope to hear from your college student more frequently than he will write or call. And you will have to send packages to college more frequently than you expected. Some advice follows which can help you be a good scout and "Be Prepared."

Letters from home

Letters from home should be cheerful; don't go into big lectures or sermons. Be chatty, encouraging, and show confidence. Do *not* dwell on Aunt Berniece's gallstones and the obituary notices.

Try to write a couple of times a week so that something is in the mailbox from time to time. It helps to address and stamp a bunch of envelopes ahead of time so one is ready to stick stuff in as you have it—bank deposit slip, photo, church bulletin, band deposit slip, news clippings, cartoons, and bank deposit slip.

If you have more than one child away from home photocopy the letter and add personal notes to each.

If your child turns out to be the one in the state who writes frequently, it is fun to keep the letters in a folder and give them as a college graduation gift. They will be fun to read again and will no doubt cause lots of laughs and memories. It would be wise not to make this decision until you see how often the letters come, as a file folder with two letters in it is a depressing sight. One could include the long distance phone bill print out as proof of communication, however.

Phone calls

Catching your child in the dorm room is next to impossible unless you have previously arranged a time for you to call. When you repeatedly call and get no answer, you will worry. You will try to call early in the morning and late at night, and then your imagination will go crazy. Where is he at this hour? Should I call the police?

A telephone answering machine is most helpful. You can hear his voice once in awhile even if it is recorded. You also can suggest, nay demand, that he call you "this very night."

There will come a time when you need to discuss another petty annoyance: never put your mom "on hold" when she calls you long-distance!

Sometimes you will receive calls which leave you feeling helpless. Examples:

"I'm stranded in Atlanta."

"The wheel came off the car on the interstate."

"I'm sick."

"I lost my retainer."

"I need help with my Halloween costume."

"I haven't seen my brother on campus for two weeks and his friends are also asking about him."

"I locked my keys in the car."

"I lost my wallet."

"May I buy a yellow tuxedo?"

"I need my original social security card by Wednesday."

"Do we have a fifty gallon cardboard drum at home?"

Investigate the possibility of conference calls with several family members once in a while if you have kids or other relatives in different parts of the country. Sometimes this is simply fun, and sometimes it helps arrive at a consensus quickly when family decisions need to be made.

Sending things

Expect all kinds of weird requests for stuff from home. In February, your pride and joy will call on Tuesday night for you to resurrect and send a pair of white shorts for the Hawaiian party on Saturday. Or you will need to dig out the old book of poems immediately for an assignment.

Have a good stock of sturdy boxes (in assorted sizes), brown paper, tape, and address labels on hand. Check the hours, pick up points, and regulations for the post office, Federal Express, United Parcel

Beverly Parks Faaborg and Tony Faaborg

Service, and other delivery services before you need them. Be sure your son or daughter knows what to do on the other end: will they need to sign for packages? Will they have access to the postal box on weekends?

Dare to be unique

Occasionally do something unexpected. Get a yam or other fun food and use markers for everyone in the family to sign it before mailing it to your son or daughter at college. Your child will be the only kid on the floor with an autographed yam. The yam will also be a starting point for conversation when you visit the campus. "Oh, you're the Yam Mother!"

Send something to recognize every holiday. Let your imagination be your guide for the unusual ones such as Ground Hog Day, St. Patrick's Day, Winter Solstice, Beethoven's Birthday (December 16).

A lot of organizations take orders for finals week goodie baskets and "Care Packages." These organizations fill a basket or box with fruit, crackers, fun little prizes or snack items and deliver the packages to students prior to the final exam week. The groups do this as a fundraiser by contacting parents ahead of time with information about orders.

A Care Package from home before final exams is a good time to show your student that you are thinking about him. You can of course also send food, something fun to wear, appropriate posters for the room, or a few dollars for a pizza break. Food from home, homemade or otherwise, is always appreciated.

A very private note to parents

When grade slips arrive, you should not open them. Some say that you can steam them open using a microwave, but holding them up almost touching a 100-watt light bulb will allow you to see through most envelopes. You have not lowered yourself to opening someone's mail, but you will be able to find out what you want to know. Beware: can you live with your conscience?

Be a pessimist

If you expect the worst in all cases, then you will be relieved and pleased when things turn out better than the worst. Prepare yourself for receiving one letter all semester and then you will rejoice when you receive four. Expect that he will have to go to summer school four times and then you will be jubilant when he has to go only twice. Prepare yourself that he is flunking everything and then you will celebrate when he gets C's and D's. Got the idea?

Polls show need to understand

My research has shown that parents are not satisfied with the number of calls and letters from students away at college. (At any rate, that is what a survey of my friends Nina and Janice revealed.)

Parents must not take personally the lack of communication with the home front. There is so much going on at college that time does get away, while at home there is a noticeable hole left by the student who is away. Resist the temptation to say you are not writing until you hear; after all, you are the mature grown-up and he is the child.

Another thing, do not "read between the lines." If the letter says, "there is not much to relate," avoid imagining that there really are things going on which he cannot relate to his parents. You might use the rule advisors use: Don't ask the question if you won't like the answer.

If you really become concerned after not being able to make contact, by all means call the college switchboard and ask for the dorm office. Then ask for the Resident Assistant (RA) for "third floor, Carver House" or whatever. You can discuss your plight with the RA who will look into the matter.

Just remember that one way we know that we have been successful at helping our children become independent is when they do not lean on us as much, so bask in how successful you are now!

Beverly Parks Faaborg and Tony Faaborg

Chapter 10
My Son, The Graduate
(exiting college)

When the day finally comes for college graduation, there will be great rejoicing, pumping of hands, dancing about, and sighing with relief. Parents are like that.

Some students want to skip the ceremony, but we recommend going through it. Like other rituals in life, this one is a celebration and a closure. Besides, parents have paid thousands of dollars for a picture of you in your cap and gown and also you might want a tassel to dangle from your car mirror with the fuzzy dice.

We have gone full circle in this book and now are back to a "wrapping up" chapter—this time wrapping up college.

Update the file folder

You should have all of your important information already together as we suggested in chapter one. Now you need to make sure it has everything from college days that you need for heading out into the world:

- College transcript
- College diploma
- Names and addresses of people who will write reference letters for you
- Names, permanent home addresses of college friends
- Awards, honors, scholarships
- Names, addresses, dates of employers during college
- Offices, committees, activities during college
- College loan information

Insure yourself

After you graduate, you almost certainly will not be covered by your parents' insurance. A phone call to insurance agents (preferably prior to graduation) will answer questions such as:

- Medical and health—May I buy continuous coverage for a few months from the same policy my parents have? Does another company sell cheaper temporary policies for people between-jobs?
- Life—Do I need more coverage now due to student loan responsibilities, auto purchase, and so forth?
- Personal belongings—Is my stuff still covered on my parents' policy while I am moving home and getting settled in my new career?
- Car—How long am I covered on my parents' policy? If I get my own car, what insurance will I need?

Money matters

There are big decisions to make in the areas of auto, apartment, clothes, and repaying loans. If you do not have an established credit rating, now is the time to work on that by buying some of your things and paying them off quickly.

You will begin to receive offers for credit cards, loans, and discounts on autos as you near college graduation. Be careful about getting into debt!

If you need to apply for a sizable loan, the bank might want someone to "co-sign" with you. You and this co-signer must remember that if you fail to pay back the loan, then the other person is liable. (Lots of people think a co-signer is merely "vouching for" the borrower. Untrue.)

You *can* go home again

Often there is a space of time when the new graduate is in limbo. Sometimes it is while job hunting. At other times, you will have a job or a military assignment waiting, but you will have some weeks or months until the paychecks start coming.

A logical (cheap) conclusion to come to is that your old room is still available at home. Your parents will enjoy getting reacquainted and having you around. Well, at least temporarily...

Go back and read the section of this book about going home during breaks and summers! The same courtesies and cautions apply.

You will again have some storage decisions to make. All of that college stuff you collected will have to find a home, and you will need to sort it, box it up for the attic or your new apartment, or else get rid of it. Do not put off this task!

One new graduate decided to follow a plan of going through three boxes each day. When he fell behind by seventy five boxes, his mom started making threats like "no supper till the boxes are sorted." Things can turn nasty.

The world is yours

Well, here you are all grown up and graduated. What an exciting time of life! You and your parents are still on speaking terms. You are confident and yet still a bit apprehensive. How wonderful to be able to say to others, *"You can survive college—we did!"*

Notes to Parents

Before you read further, make sure your child is really going to leave college. There are a lot of "perpetual students" out there and you could have one. These students keep going back for more—more majors, more certifications, more degrees. Somehow they never finish with college, so ask the big question: are you going to graduate school now??

What a sense of pride you will have as you watch your graduate receiving his diploma! For some families, it marks the time when the child has passed the parents in the field of education. It may mean that the child will out-earn the parents. It could be that the child will have a title or initials after his name.

At any rate, it means that "we as a family made it!" All of the little rough spots will fade in time and all that remains will be the sense of accomplishment that the whole family will feel.

Grandma and Grandpa will begin to ask about gift ideas for the college graduate. Again, you are prepared. Some of the same gift ideas are suitable for college graduation that you saw in the Wrapping Up High School chapter. Things like dictionaries and towels wear out while things like luggage and briefcases need updating.

Graduation gift ideas

Automotive
car
car paint job
car accessories
telephone
membership in auto club
insurance premium payment
tool kit
first aid kit
small shovel
emergency survival kit
atlas
coveralls
gloves
spare gas can
jumper cables
tire pressure gauge
instant tire inflator
fire extinguisher
reflective warning triangle
citizens band radio

Books
etiquette book
cookbook
medical reference
handyman guide
Bible
car owner reference
subscriptions

Wardrobe
update for career needs
sewing kit

Apartment Items
pay rent
household insurance premium payment
telephone
appliances
dishes
linens
closet organizers
vacuum
sleeping bag
tool kit
first aid kit

Apartment Items (cont.)
games (Monopoly, checkers,
    horseshoes)
laundry items
folding clothes dryer rack
extension cord

Hobby Items
sports interests (golf, ski, photo)
camping equipment
music equipment
electronic equipment

Sentimental
college ring
jewelry
family tree information
family address book
scrapbook
family photo album
letter of love
collection of letters written home
    during college
pocket watch
collection of childhood papers
frame special childhood drawing
mount/display awards from scouts,
    sports, and so forth

Other
trip
money
stocks and bonds
luggage
gift certificate (restaurant, store,
    motel, recreation)
membership in club (country club,
    golf club, YM/YWCA)
health insurance premium payment
life insurance premium payment
tool kit
trunk
medicine chest
key ring
money clip
business card case
personalized stationery, business cards

Sources of additional information:

American Trade Schools Directory. Jericho, NY: Croner Publications, Inc. 34 Jericho Turnpike (11753).

Campus Visits and College Interviews. New York, NY: College Board Publications, PO Box 886 (10101).

College Costbook. New York, NY: College Board Publications, PO Box 886 (10101).

Peterson's Four-year Colleges. Princeton, NJ: Peterson's Guides.

Peterson's Guide to College Admissions. Princeton, NJ: Peterson's Guides.

Costs and financial aid at over 1,700 colleges...

Peterson's 1991 College Money Handbook. Princeton, NJ: Peterson's Guides.

Federal assistance programs...

The Student Guide. Washington, DC: Department of Education, 400 Maryland Ave. SW (20202).

Scholarships, fellowships, grants, and loans...

The College Blue Book. New York, NY: Macmillan Publications, 866 Third Ave. (10022).

Writing college enterance essays...

Bauld, H. (1987). *On Writing the College Application Essay.* New York, NY: Harper and Row, 10 East 53rd St. (10022).

College entrance interviews...

Utterback, A.S. (1984). *College Admissions Face to Face.* Washington, DC: Transemantics, Inc. 1601 Connecticut Ave. NW (20009).

Guides to two and four year colleges...

College Handbook. New York, NY: Guidance Publishing. The College Board, 45 Columbus Ave. (10023).

Fields of study and schools offering the programs...

Index of Majors. New York, NY: College Board Publications, PO Box 886 (10101).